The Twerp Generation
Growing Up In Dallas in The '50's and '60's

By Richard Parker

The Twerp Generation
Growing Up In Dallas in The '50's and '60's

by Richard Parker

Published by Oomph Media, LLC
Fort Worth, Texas

First Printing 2012

Printed in the United States of America

Dedicated to Bill Camfield – aka "Icky Twerp"
(Pictured on the front cover and first page)

Contents

—

4

National Television
Including: Roy and Dale, Captain Video, Superman, Ozzie and Harriett, *Ding Dong School*, Howdy Doody, *The Mickey Mouse Club*, Beany and Cecil, "Plunk your magic twanger, Froggy" and a lot more.

Life In Dallas in the 60's
Including: Stores and shopping, 60's flashbacks, Six Flags, Top 40 Radio, Movies made in Dallas, The Lewisville Pop Festival, the Lady of the Lake and a lot more.

Dallas at the Movies
Including every movie theater in Dallas in the 50s and 60s – indoor and drive-ins. Plus our favorite teen flicks of the era.

Sports Report – The 60's
Including: The Cowboys vs. The Texans.

The Restaurants We Loved
Including: Kip's, Lucas B&B, favorite burger hangouts, Joe Moseley's, The Dairyette, Sivil's, Brockles, and a feast of others.

Three Chords and a Cloud of Dust – The Dallas Music Scene in the 60's
The clubs, the bands and the records. The Studio Club, The roller rink rock-and-roll connection, high school hops and a lot more.

101 Boomer Things To Know About Dallas
I didn't actually count them. Could be more, could be less. Who's counting?

—

5

Introduction

This book is intentionally a "hodge-podge". Because we will cover hundreds and hundreds of seemingly unrelated subjects, there is really no way to put it into a standard history book format. Anyway, it's not about history – not in a technical 'school-bookish' sort of way. It's about memories. It's about the way the historical facts that will be presented make us all *feel*.

Some of the stories will be presented in a narrative "story format". Some will be collected in simple short paragraphs; a few will only appear in brief bullet points.

If it is history at all it is the Pop Culture History of what happened while we were growing up in and around the cities of Dallas and Fort Worth, Texas way back in the 1950s and 1960s. Bits and pieces of our collective memories. Like watching a thousand short video clips of our childhood.

There will be an equal dose of foolishless for every fact presented. There will be just as many 'wasn't that wonderful?' moments as there will be 'what were we thinking?' moments.

There will also be as many photos and graphics as we can squeeze in, since we boomers are a very visual generation.

There will be no test when it's all over. Hopefully there *will* be a warm glow of recognition of the kid you used to be.

The Pre-1950 Years In Dallas

Prior to 1840 – The area was inhabited primarily by Native Americans including the Anadarko and Caddo tribes. Occasional traders from Mexico would visit the area. Then a bunch of other stuff happened. But since we promised that this was not going to be an actual history lesson, we're just gonna breeze through it all. So hold on. (Those opposed to learning anything actually historical, flip a few pages forward.) Warning some of the stuff below I just made up, but most of it is somewhat true, like it matters.

1841:
　　Dallas is founded and named by John Neely Bryan. The Peters Colony, a settlers' group, arrives and settles near Dallas.

1849:
　　The first newspaper, The Cedar Snag, later changed to The Dallas Herald debuted. The headline was something about a goat.

<u>1850 - 1855</u>:
Dallas, with a population of over 400, is named the county seat of Dallas County. The first bridge over the Trinity River is built by Alexander Cockrell, who later apparently also owned a hill, 'cause there is a Cockrell Hill around these parts somewhere, but so what?
In a city-wide election, Dallas came within 28 votes of being named "Hord's Ridge". ("The Hord's Ridge Cowboys"??? Somehow it wouldn't have been the same.)

<u>1855 - 1860</u>:
La Reunion, settlers from France, Switzerland and Belgium settled near what is now called Reunion Plaza.
Dallas was officially incorporated as a city and the first mayor elected. The population of Dallas was under 2000. A fire destroyed much of the city. What a drag. They went so much trouble to build it.

<u>1861 – 1865</u>:
Future OK Corral gunfighter Billy Clanton was born in Dallas. Something called "The Civil War" happened but since TV was not yet invented, most folks in Texas missed it.

<u>1870 – 1880</u>:
Firsts in Dallas – volunteer fire company, train service, E.M. Kahn store, Sanger Brothers store, opera, telephone, wrong number dialed, and baseball team.
Also in the decade, Doc Holiday killed a guy in Dallas and hotfooted it west. Local train robber, Sam Bass, was tracked down and killed near Dallas.

—

1880 – 1890:

The Dallas Brown Stockings baseball team won the Texas League Championship. Land in Dallas was going for $15 an acre, and your great-grandfather didn't buy any of it. The Dallas Morning News began publication. The Texas State Fair was organized in Dallas. Dallas was the largest city in Texas.

1890 – 1900:

The "Old Red" Courthouse was completed, still standing in downtown Dallas today.

The first motion picture ever to play in Dallas was seen in a demonstration of Thomas Edison's Vitascope System at the Dallas Opera House (no popcorn was served, so it may not count as an official movie event. However two teenagers *were* caught necking in the balcony, so I say it's official.)

The first automobile arrived in Dallas and promptly ran into something.

1900 – 1910:

Annie Oakley and Buffalo Bill Cody brought their Wild West Show to the Texas State Fair in Dallas. The Andrew Carnegie Dallas Public Library opened. Oak Cliff was annexed into Dallas. Neiman-Marcus Department Store opened and someone was overcharged on the very first day. The Trinity River flooded leaving four thousand homeless. President William Howard Taft visited the State Fair in Dallas.

Annie Oakley and Buffalo Bill Cody

<u>1910 – 1920</u>:
The first airplane flew over Dallas. The Dallas Symphony Orchestra was formed. The Adolphus Hotel opened and someone checked in as "Mr. and Mrs. John Smith", a likely story. The Houston Street Viaduct opened, connecting Oak Cliff to Dallas. The Marsalis Zoo opened with two squirrels and a june bug named "Ralphie". (No. not really!).

Love Field opened as an army training facility. Southern Methodist University began and was already acting snooty. Union Station opened in downtown and the first train was late. The War facility known as Camp Dick began at Fair Park. The soldiers were not allowed to ride the rides.

Love Field during World War I

1920 – 1930: Dallas becomes forty-second largest city in the U.S. WRR signed on as the first radio station in Texas The Majestic Theater opened, marking the beginning of the "Elm Street Theater Row." The Magnolia Building was built. At 29 stories high, it was considered to be the tallest building west of the Mississippi until the early forties.

WBAP and WFAA radio stations signed on within a month of each other. Discovered by Paramount Records while performing in Deep Ellum, Blind Lemon Jefferson became the biggest selling blues recording artist in the U.S. Charles Lindbergh landed at Love Field and rode in a parade through town. The convenience store industry was born in Oak Cliff. The first store eventually spawned the worldwide 7-Eleven chain. Unfortunately everyone had to wait about 40 more years for the first Slurpee.

Dallas skyline in 1927

1930 - Bonnie Parker and Clyde Barrow met in Dallas. Ah, young love.

1931 – 1940:

Bonnie and Clyde were killed in Louisiana, so much for young love! My Great-Uncle Hugh Fitzgerald (then the sheriff of Ellis County) was in the posse sent to kill Bonnie and Clyde in Louisiana. The posse had split into two groups in order to cover either road that the bandits might take. My Uncle Hugh was in the wrong group. He heard all the gunshots, but never got to take one himself. To his dying day this was his biggest regret in life.

"The Flying Red Horse" was placed atop the Magnolia Building. In downtown Dallas, the city's first parking meter was installed, the first parking ticket issued and the first parking ticket fix occurred, all within a week of each other.

White Rock Lake froze over, hell did not.

The opening of The Texas Centennial was attended by President Franklin D. Roosevelt. Fair Park was refurbished for the Centennial. A dancer named "Corrine The Apple Girl" stripped naked at sideshow and the Fair attendance rose dramatically. (See article below.)

The Apple of Anybody's Eye

MLLE. CORRINE AND NAT RODGERS.

Mademoiselle Corrine, blond "apple" dancer for the "Streets of All Nations" show, who arrived in Dallas Thursday with Ernie Young, impresario of the attraction, and Mrs. Young is shown above as she stepped from the train, receiving her wardrobe from that master costumer, Nat D. Rodgers, managing director of the Streets of All Nations.

Mr. Young, who has brought many of his attractions to Dallas in recent years, also brought with him sixty entertainers for his show, which will start rehearsals Friday night at the Centennial area.

<u>1941 – 1950</u>:

The Fair Park Bandshell became the site for the premier of The Starlight Operettas and World War Two started – the two events reportedly unconnected.

The Dallas location of the Ford Motor plant is converted to war-effort production, making primarily military trucks and jeeps. Dallas institutes a war rationing program. The Dallas landmark, the Dr Pepper Plant opened on Mockingbird Lane.

Construction began on Central Expressway and continues to this day whenever I try to drive on it.

The author of this book was born, along with a few less notables. WBAP began TV broadcasting in Fort Worth and KRLD-TV became the first television station in Dallas, followed shortly by KBTS-TV (later WFAA).

Which brings us neatly to…1950!

We Go Boom

Although the boomers officially began arriving in the mid-40s with the end of World War II, we begin our saga in 1950 – the first year of the first boomistic decade.

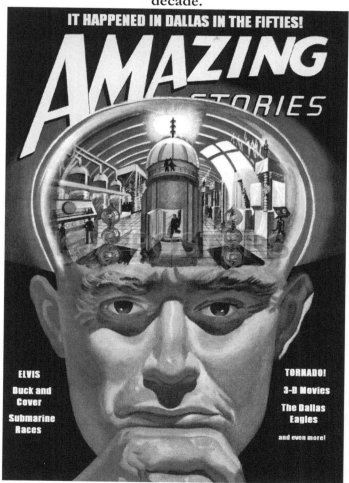

In Dallas In The 1950's

Population of Dallas in 1950 – 434,462
Population at the end of the decade – 679,684

A Roast Prime Rib of Beef dinner at Wyatt's Cafeteria was 70¢. The New Years Day "black-eyed peas and hog jowls" special was only 39¢ which is about 40¢ more than I woulda paid. (1950)

In 1950, 90¢ would buy a ticket to the Dallas Symphony Orchestra's performance of George Gershwin's works.

A brand new 1951 Austin at Clarence Talley Autos was $1395. If that was too steep, you could get a used Chevy for $75.

Colgate Tooth Powder cost 29¢ at Ward's Cut Rate Drugs. (1952)

In downtown Dallas the top movie price on Saturday night at the Majestic Theater was 70¢. (1954)

A brick home on Desdemona in the Casa View area sold for under $10,000. (1954)

The required Dallas Independent School District elementary school writing tablet called "We Draw To Write" cost a dime. (1954)

At the Casa Linda Theater a box of Root Beer Barrels candy cost a nickel. (1955)

In the late '50's blues legend Jimmy Reed performed at Teen Timers in Casa Linda for a 25¢ admission. The opening act was The Nightcaps. All for a quarter!

In 1950 a Dallas stenographer could expect to earn around $35 a week.

In 1952 there were 110 traffic deaths in Dallas.

In 1957 a copy of Gene Vincent's national hit record *Lotta Lovin'* (which was recorded at Sellers Recording Studio in downtown Dallas) would cost you 79¢ at The Dallasan Record Store.

Telephone numbers had a word prefix (like Davis 7-3933. Others included Lakeside, Riverside, Broadway, Diamond and Taylor.)

The State Fair featured: Elsie The Cow, The Cotton Club Revue, Fletcher's Corny Dogs, Jack's French Fries, The Ride-N-Laff, The Comet Coaster, The Cuddle Up, The Caterpillar and The Bubble Bounce.

KBTV became WFAA-TV in 1950

Also at the fair: Monkey Auto Races, The Alligator Man, Dunk 'Em Booth and Penny Arcade.

October 3, 1954 – Guitarist Stevie Ray Vaughan was born in Dallas.

Two years before the Dallas Cowboys kicked off, real cowboys were riding in Mesquite. The Mesquite Rodeo opened its chutes for the first time in 1958.

In the fifties, Wyatt's was not only "DeLuxe" but "in your neighborhood."

On April 2, 1957 this very tornado roared through Dallas, threatening the parking lot shown above. While in town the tornado also tore up a bunch of other stuff. The tornado centered on Oak Cliff, which was really uncalled for since that area was full of very nice folks who deserved better. The twister ripped through homes and businesses, killing ten people and injuring two hundred. The twister was one of the first anywhere to be filmed by newsreel cameras from many angles. These films later served as major educational tools for those studying violent weather.

The First Animated TV Commercial

"7 days a week we open up at seven
And 7 days a week we're open 'til eleven
From 7 'til 11, from 7 'til 11.
We've got ice, drinks, milk, cheese
Meat, fish, bread, peas.
From soup to nuts, that's why we sing
7-Eleven's got everything!"

7 A.M. ROOSTER   11 P.M. OWL

This is said to be the first animated TV commercial in America and it was produced in Dallas. The famous 7-Eleven "owl and rooster" singing cartoon commercial for Dallas' own chain of convenience stores, opened the floodgates for scores of singing, dancing television cartoon pitchmen for decades to come.

April 16, 1955 – Elvis Presley appeared on The Big D Jamboree for the first time. He made several appearances on the show during the year including on September 3rd advertised on the flyer below.

At the time of that appearance, Elvis' current record release was *Mystery Train / I Forgot To Remember To Forget* on the Sun label out of Memphis.

Earlier in the year, Elvis auditioned to be on Arthur Godfrey's Talent Scouts, but was rejected. Apparently they weren't very good at scouting talent.

Rats! Foiled Again!

Yes, there really was a "gang" called The Lakewood Rats in Dallas in the 50s. The word "gang" may be way too strong however, as the legendary group's rowdy reputation may have become exaggerated during the years. Some Dallasites remember them as merely a colorfully named social club. Will the real Lakewood Rats please stand up and be identified?

Lakewood Rats Crash Dance, Eat Goodies, Beat Up Guests

Police Sunday were hunting nearly a dozen Northeast Dallas youths of high school age who broke up a private dance at the Lee Park community house, beating up several young male guests at the dance with blackjacks, knucks and other weapons.

The group of youths holding the party noticed about 11 p.m. that a group of eight or ten youths who drove up in an old jaloppy had joined the party and were eating and drinking all the refreshments.

When the uninvited guests were asked to leave they began fighting, and police were called to quell the disturbance, but the intruders fled before their arrival.

Youths at the party told officers the crashers were a group of toughs known as the Lakewood Rats, and several of the boys in the gang were identified. The Lakewood Rats have been involved in several gang fights in recent months.

In 1958 researchers at Texas Instruments in Dallas invented the integrated circuit. This allowed for the growth of the electronics industry and the introduction of the personal computer.

Often described as the first fully enclosed and covered shopping mall in America, Big Town opened in Mesquite just east of Dallas, in 1959

22

Stickers on the rear window of Ford cars manufactured in the Ford Plant on East Grand Avenue read "Built In Texas By Texans"

Akard Street in the mid-fifties looking toward the Adolphus Hotel.

23

People and Places

Hamilton Park, a suburb in North Dallas, was created in 1954 and named for Dallas African-American doctor and civic leader, Dr. Richard T. Hamilton.

Justin Ford Kimball died in Dallas on October 7, 1956. He was a Dallas educator and the founder of the Blue Cross insurance plan. In 1958 Kimball High School was named in his honor.

In 1956, The Great State Fair of Texas featured Elvis Presley, the brand new Monorail (it was a miraculous new mode of transportation) and comedian Victor Borge.

Broadway comedy star Bobby Clark was starring in "Damn Yankees" at the Music Hall.

And I got sick after eating too much junk food and threw up on the Ferris Wheel.

Another great year at The Fair.

The Dallas Drought

From 1951 until 1957 a serious drought gripped Dallas and the North Texas area. Area lakes were drained and water rationing became essential. Approximately 70 million gallons of water were used in the city in 1951, which was successfully reduced to 42 million gallons the next year in spite of a population growth. During this time, area residents could amuse themselves by walking across White Rock Lake and even picnicking at the lake's center.

By the end of 1952 the water shortage was critical; Lake Dallas for instance held only 11 percent of its capacity. Streams only trickled or dried up completely. In 1956, the final year of the drought, the Bonnie Barge cruise boat was high and dry as conditions completely dried up White Rock Lake (see photo below.)

Dry Humor

During the mid-fifties drought, a desperate Dallas City Council actually hired a rainmaker to try and bring rainfall. The moisture monarch was named Dr. Irving P. Krick and he was paid over $36,000 by the city in 1952.

The annual droughts became so bad that the city rationed drinking water. I remember as a 9 year old standing in line at a dispensing location near Norbuck Park with my mother to fill the single gallon jug they allowed us per day. My folks and I actually walked to the very center of White Rock Lake in the summer of '56. I was shocked not only by the dry, broken dirt under our feet, but by how shallow the lake would have been even if it were full.

The natural tragedy led to positive long-term solutions with the plans to create the Lewisville Dam, and Lakes Tawakoni, Ray Hubbard and Aubrey. In 1956 the rains returned filling the new and existing lakes and by 1957 the drought had ended.

But when it rains, it pours, and that prayed-for 1957 rainfall not only filled the lakes again but caused severe flooding in our area.

- Dallas News Staff Photo

WHITE ROCK LAKE GETS A CLEANING

The drouth has exposed parts of White Rock Lake along the north and east shores that have not been uncovered since the city quit using it for a water supply twelve years ago. Monday, park department crews began clearing these areas where fishermen wade of cans, glass, automobile tires, fenders and other debris. Work will proceed farther out as the level drops while the city taps the lake as an emergency water supply. L. M. Cameron, Ray Barnett and Maple Powell, left to right, are removing some of the debris so hazardous to fishermen and boats.

—Dallas News Staff Photo by Jack Beers.

WHITE ROCK LAKE BECOMING DESERT OF SILT

Skeletons of sunken boats, now high and dry on the exposed bottom of White Rock Lake, starkly disclose the condition of the lake after years of siltation and drouth. The lake's level now is about six feet below spillway level because of lack of rain and withdrawals to supplement the city's water supply until rains come and fill the major supply lakes. Heavy siltation over the years has shrunk White Rock greatly, and the Park Board is planning to restore badly silted parts when the city no longer needs the water.

Pure Water Promised By Hauling If Needed

Citizens Charter Association candidates for the City Council Sunday promised Dallas pure water for drinking and cooking even if it means hauling water to homes with a gigantic fleet of trucks.

Eight members of the nine-man CCA slate took the pure-water pledge after studying a joint report, compiled by six firms of engineers, on Dallas' water plight.

The eight men met in the office of Mayor Candidate R. L. Thornton at the Mercantile National Bank. The ninth candidate, Roderic B. Thomas, was out of town.

"We will exhaust every means available to avoid the use of West Fork water," the candidates said in a joint statement.

Many Dallas residents have expressed alarm at the idea of drinking water from the polluted West Fork of the Trinity River, fearing it would be unsafe even after extensive purification measures.

"If the (West Fork) water is ruled unfit for cooking and drinking purposes it certainly can be used for fire prevention and for sanitary purposes," said the candidates' statement. "With an ample supply of artesian water available for drinking and cooking, we will haul by truck or by tank sufficient pure artesian well water for cooking and drinking."

The report of the engineers pointed out that water was hauled to Dallas homes in the 1908-1912 drouth; and to Fort Worth homes following the flood there in 1949.

The candidates, after studying the engineers' report, agreed that it "clearly and factually presents the emergency water situation as it affects Dallas at this time."

The engineers termed the water situation grave, but added there is no reason for great alarm over the possibility of Dallas being without enough pure water for drinking and cooking.

The engineers listed these figures:

About 500,000 persons are served by the Dallas water system.

The city normally uses 120 gallons per person each day. Most of this is for sanitation, air conditioning, lawn sprinkling and industrial use.

Under a dire emergency we could get along on twenty gallons or less per person daily for domestic purposes (that is, for drinking and cooking).

This means that Dallas' pure-water requirements amount to only 10,000,000 gallons per day. The city has an assured supply of at least twice that much pure well water—20,000,000 gallons a day.

The Sports Report

Texans For A Year

Eight years before the Cowboys, the National Football League established a franchise in Dallas. At least for a few games in 1952. Known as the Dallas Texans (not to be confused with the American Football League Dallas Texans of the early sixties), this team boasted a proud record of eleven losses and only one victory. Faced with near empty stands and almost complete fan apathy, the team left Dallas in mid-season. The team then moved to Baltimore at the end of that first season, where they became known as The Colts. In 1984 The Colts bolted again, this time to Indianapolis.

The Man With The Eagle Eye

Richard Burnett, the owner of The Dallas Eagles baseball team and Burnett Field, built the team to a Texas League powerhouse. In the decade they won three Texas League championships.

Burnett will also be remembered for integrating the Texas League when in 1952, when he added African American pitcher David Hoskins to the team.
Burnett Field, located along present day I-35 hosted games with such teams as The Houston Buffaloes, The Tulsa Oilers and The Austin Senators. The Eagles were   Dallas heroes from 1948 until 1960 when the team merged with perennial rivals The Fort Worth Cats, becoming The

Dallas-Fort Worth Rangers. (Although the names are the same, there is no relation between this team and the later Texas Rangers.) Eventually the team was dissolved.

In the fifties: The Fort Worth Cats and the Dallas Eagles. Quite a regional rivalry.

Gridiron Greats

At SMU the charismatic young quarterback Don Meredith was named All-American in 1958 and 1959. Other Mustang standouts of the decade were Kyle Rote, Forrest Gregg, Fred Benners and Raymond Berry.

Little Mo

Maureen "Little Mo" Connolly, longtime Dallas resident and wife of restaurateur Norman Brinker was the outstanding female tennis player in the world during the fifties. She won the U.S. Women's Tennis Championship in 1951, 1952 and 1953 and captured the women's Wimbledon Titles in 1952, 1953 and 1954. She was voted Associated Press "Female Athlete of the Year" in 1952, 1953 and 1954.

Dallas Open Starts Swinging

Preceded by the Dallas Centennial Open in 1956, The Dallas Open golf tournament began officially in 1957. Sam Snead won the first two competitions followed by Julius Boros in 1959.

Cotton Bowl Game Results For The Decade

1950 – Rice over North Carolina 27 - 13
1951 – Tennessee over Texas 20 - 14
1952 – Kentucky over TCU 20 – 7
1953 – Texas over Tennessee 16 – 0
1954 – Rice over Alabama 28 – 6
1955 – Georgia Tech over Arkansas 14 – 6
1956 – Mississippi over TCU 14 – 13
1957 – TCU over Syracuse 28 – 27
1958 – Navy over Rice 20 – 7
1959 – TCU tied Air Force 0 – 0

Roller Derby and Wrestling

TV phenomenons, these "sporting events" caught the public fancy in the fifties. Wrestling stars like "Gorgeous George" and Roller Derby rollers like "Charley O", Joanie Weston, Ann Cavello and "Big Red" Annis Jensen became superstars for a brief period.

The Roller Derby programs usually featured the super team of the sport The Bay Area Bombers, and were originally broadcast from Kezar Pavilion in Oakland. The Bombers went up against teams like The New York Chiefs, The Los Angeles Thunderbirds and The Ohio Jolters.

Then locally, our "Texas Westerners" were usually rolling against our dreaded rivals from San Francisco – The Bay Area Bombers. These were broadcast on Channel 11 from Fort Worth's North Side Coliseum. Other teams such as The Midwest Pioneers and the California Cardinals would occasionally appear at Memorial Auditorium in Dallas

Wrestling

KRLD Channel 4 was the home for Tuesday Night Wrestling from the Sportatorium in the fifties and then "Studio Wrestling" on Saturday afternoons in the late 50's and 60's. Studio Wrestling was exactly that - wrestling matches staged in a TV studio exclusively for the TV viewer. A small studio audience on three sides of the ring gave the show an air of a live sporting event. Bill Mercer was the host of both of these programs.

In addition, live wrestling events were regularly promoted at Ed McLemore's Sportatorium, also the home of The Big D Jamboree (see later chapter for more information on the Jamboree.)

Dallas wrestling stars of the 50's and 60's included Fritz Von Erich, Killer Karl Kox, Duke Keomuka, Bull Curry and Cowboy Bob Ellis.

"Submarine Races" and Other Fifties Events

In the fifties, White Rock Lake continued to be a popular spot for young lovers seeking privacy. During this era two joking reasons couples gave for visiting the lake at night were to search for The Lady of The Lake and to watch "the submarine races."

Also at White Rock Lake, three long-established locations were available for private parties. The Dreyfuss Club, Winfrey Point and The Big Thicket had been at the lakefront for several years, and during the 1950s each saw a continuing parade of parties, reunions, weddings and receptions.

In the fifties, The Skyline Beauty Salon in Dallas offered a new hairstyle inspired by current TV stars. It was called "The Poodle-Do".

In the mid-50s KLIF 1190 placed DJ Buddy McGregor on top of a flagpole where he broadcast live during his marathon event. Although flagpole sitting wasn't new this was apparently the first time it was done by a radio personality who broadcast from the perch.

3-D Movies

The first 3-Dimensional film to hit theaters was *Bwana Devil* in 1952. Once audiences became used to the 3-D glasses, the impact of visuals that seemed to come at you from the screen caught on with moviegoers around the world. Other 3-D movies of the era included: *House of Wax, The Creature From The Black Lagoon* and *Kiss Me Kate*. There is a lot more about movies and theaters in Dallas in a later chapter of this book.

A couple of fun ways to spend the day in the Fifties... Vickery Park and Jupiter Bowl on Garland Road.

To us the decade of the fifties was the time for...
Fizzies
Davy Crockett coonskin caps
Hula hoops
Grapette Soda
Lincoln Logs
Bo Diddley
PF Fliers
Fearless Fosdick
Betsy Wetsy
Duane Eddy
Beehive hairdos
Green Stamps
3 speed Hi-Fi record players
Metal ice cubes trays with levers to loosen the ice
School tests printed on smelly mimeograph paper
Beany and Cecil
Rootie Kazootie
Icky Twerp
Roller-skate keys
Cap guns
The Fuller Brush Man
45 rpm records
Candy cigarettes
Little wax bottles with flavoring inside
Soft drink machines with real glass bottles
Colorful aluminum drinking glasses
Coffee shops with jukeboxes right at the table
Home milk delivery in glass bottles
Spoolies
Golden Nectar flavor Kool Aid
Living room furniture shaped like flying saucers
Telephone party lines
Newsreels and cartoons before the movie

There Are Places We Remember...

Wee St. Andrews Miniature Golf
Storybook Land
Sandy Lake Park
The Varsity Shop
Goff's Hamburgers
Sivil's Drive In
Charcos Hamburgers
The Prince of Hamburgers
Tietze Pool
The Science Museum at Fair Park
Bob-O-Links
Jupiter Bowl
Cabell's Convenience Stores
Southern Maid vs. Lone Star Donuts
Skillern's Drug Stores
Flag Pole Hill

Below: Tietze Park Pool - the 50s.

The Big Thicket
The Dreyfus Club
Winfrey Point
Pig Stands
Vickery Park
McCree Pool
The Harry Stone
Pool
The White Rock
Paddle Boats
Ashburn's and Polar Bear Ice Cream stores
The Devil's Bowl and Green Valley Raceway
The Bronco Bowl
Burnett Field
The Cotton Bowling Palace

Do You Remember...

Storybook Land?

Did your folks ever take you to Storybook Land? It was opened on April 15, 1956 and was a kid-friendly paradise for several years in the Dallas area. Mr. and Mrs. K.K. Stanfield designed and operated the park which was located in Irving on Highway 183.

On opening day 10,000 paying customers visited the park. Storybook Land had only one ride but it was a doozie - A Merry-Go-Round with real live horses (Shetland Ponies actually). Within a few months another themed park opened next door to Storybook Land. Called "Cowboy Town" it was the forerunner to Six Flags' Wild West section. It featured live shoot-outs, hourly bank robberies and all the western action one could imagine. (Flip a few pages for more "Cowboy Town" stuff.)

Below: Three Billy Goats Gruff with the Troll hiding under the bridge. (The goats were real - the Troll just looked real.)

Opening Today!

10 ACRES OF

FABULOUS ENTERTAINMENT!

For the Young... *at heart!*

Storybook Land

OPEN DAILY 9 A.M. 'TIL 9 P.M.

There's nothing like STORYBOOK LAND within 1,000 miles. Here you can relive with your children, the thrill of discovering never-never land where Mother Goose and all her friends live. Come and bring the Kiddies.

On Highway 183—Midway Dallas and Fort Worth

FREE PARKING—SNACK BAR

P.O. Box 446, Irving, Texas

Telephone BL-3-8538

Opening Set Sunday for Fantasyland

Ten acres of fairyland will be officially opened Sunday at 3 p.m. with a ribbon-cutting ceremony.

The place is Storybook Land, just east of Carter Field on Highway 183, and in it are buildings, animals and displays that depict many famous nursery rhymes and fairy tale characters.

Built by Mr. and Mrs. K. K. Stanfield, the miniature community of fantasy people represents an investment of about $250,000, and fulfills a life-long dream of the couple. Everything from Jack and Jill and their fateful hill to Little Boy Blue asleep at his post have been included. There is even a live skunk and black sheep.

There will be an admission charge, and inside are a refreshment house (built like one of gingerbread) selling light snacks, and a novelty shop selling souvenirs.

The front of Storybook Land has been built to resemble a castle from fairyland, complete with a drawbridge.

Above: The Grand Entrance To Storybook Land

Above: Rub a dub dub, three men in a tub.

And right down the street from Storybook Land was...
COWBOY TOWN

THERE'S A replica of the frontier called Cowboy Town out on the Fort Worth cutoff where the hired hands re-enact scenes from the Old West for the cap pistol trade.

Other day one of the teen-age "robbers" appeared on Main Street a few minutes after he had helped to hold up the stage coach ride. He was unexpectedly challenged to draw by an 8-year-old customer.

"Well, I'll draw agin you," said the robber, as he got off his horse, "but if I shoot first, you got to promise to fall down."

"That'll depend on whether you hit me," said the eight-year-old.

"Now, wait a minute! How about whether or not you hit me."

"Mister," said the 8-year-old, "I don't miss."

Cowboy Town In 3d Season

Cowboy Town, replica of a Western frontier town, located on Highway 183 midway between Dallas and Fort Worth, has launched its third season.

Hailed among Texas' most unusual amusement centers, Cowboy Town is the place where children are deputized and help maintain law and order amidst bloodless gun duels, bank robberies, stagecoach hold-ups and many other exciting events.

Sheriff Lucky is there to deputize the children and guide their activities. The show runs continuously from 11 a.m. until dark.

The fame of Cowboy Town has spread to the 49 states, even overseas. Many visitors have sent friends, relatives and visitors from afar to see "real cowboys."

During the height of the TV western days, Cowboy Town was quite a draw for local Wyatt Earp Wannabees. Kids were encouraged to bring their six-shooters and have real (kind of) gunfights with the local bad guys.

Cowboy Town also featured fun rides like an hourly stagecoach trip that somehow got held up every doggone time. There was also horseback riding, an old time carriage ride and the donkey-cart trail ride. To add to the fun, the bank was held up several times a day by rowdy desperadoes and the Sheriff kept throwing kids in the hoosegow.

41

Atomic Everything

A weird fad, as it embraced what we were most afraid of – all-out atomic war. Yet we look back fondly on movies like Atomic Monster, restaurants with names like the Atomic Café, The Miss Atom Bomb Contests, plus games, music, toys and more all with the "Atom" tag.

Bomb shelters appeared in basements and backyards across America, fully stocked with water, food and kerosene lanterns. Kids were issued military style dog tags (like those shown below) so that after we were burned up beyond recognition, future earthlings could identify our remains. It was such a cheerful decade in so many ways.

"Conelrad" became the "early warning system" in an attempt to comfort Americans with the thought that they would know in advance prior to burning to a crisp in a nuclear attack.

———

Fun comic books of the fifties.

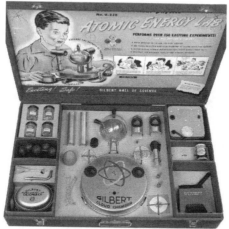

Every boy's dream – blow up the world!

Remember this?

"We interrupt this program to bring you a test of the emergency broadcasting system. If this were an actual emergency..." Of course we kids knew that in case of an actual atomic emergency we would all be crispy critters, but that didn't stop the hopeful broadcasters of Conelrad. Luckily the system was never used in a real atomic emergency. I think I would've remembered that.

It always seemed that the local TV channels picked the worst times to bust in and frighten us with their "not-actually-an-emergency" reminder that we were all going die any day now. Right in the middle of *The Roy Rogers Show* or just when Dick Clark was about to list the week's Top Ten records.

We knew it in our little hearts. We could survive that direct atom bomb hit if we were just kneeling beside our desks or huddled in the hallway. We learned this during our regular duck and cover drills at school. I was never sure if "duck and cover" would protect me anywhere other than in the school building, but still it was a good thing to know. Apparently the authorities did believe that snuggling in beside a school desk would protect one from an atomic bomb, or maybe they just enjoyed traumatizing kids.

Ducking and covering was the elementary school equivalent of wishing and hoping. "Please don't drop the bomb while I'm in this humiliating position!"

An essential in-school film called "Duck and Cover" starring "Bert The Turtle" taught kids how and why to perform the drills, while scaring us stupid at the same time. The title frame from this fear-producing film is shown above.

Of course we know now that ducking and covering would not protect us from a nuclear explosion, just burn us up while we were in that silly crouch. Nevertheless, it was good for the DISD to instill a little good old fashioned paranoia into grade school children.

Above, left: An atomic test in the fifties. On the right: The 1951 "Miss Atomic Energy" winner receives her radioactive trophy.

SIREN FOR CITY ALERT

Dallas fire inspectors D. D. Ramsey, top, and F. F. Dunaway, inspect the huge Civil Defense siren atop the downtown Central Fire Station. At 12:30 p.m. Sunday, this siren and 34 others in the city will blast forth for two four-minute intervals. It will be the first time the City-County Civil Defense Commission has ordered a citywide test of the siren alarm system.—Staff Photo.....

In 1959, the city installed Civil Defense warning sirens. Although one stated purpose was for warning of an atomic attack, the real use for the sirens was in times of tornados. And to scare the beejeebers out of folks when they tested them.

The Great State Fair of Texas

Since 1886, The State Fair of Texas has been thrilling generations of Texans, right from the heart of Dallas.

Greeted by Big Tex, the 52-foot tall talking cowboy, many millions of visitors have passed through the gates of the State Fair of Texas. To us, as kids, the Fair may have meant different things than to our parents.

What did the State Fair Mean to Boomers...?

Corny Dogs and the Comet Coaster. The Chevy Show and the Cotton Club Revue. Joie Chitwood's Auto Thrill Show. Belgian Waffles. The Penny Arcade and Youngblood's Chicken for lunch. The Million Dollar Midway. The Double Ferris Wheel and the Caterpillar Ride. The Wax Museum and the Aquarium. Stuffed Buffalo in the Museum of Natural History. The Bubble Bounce and wearing a live chameleon on your shirt. "Kiss Me I'm Irish" buttons. "Gee, it's fun to get lost" advertised on the front of the Fun House. The Alligator Man and the Monkey Lady.

The fountain at the Lagoon, this postcard
is from the mid-fifties.

Elsie the Borden Cow. Live and in person!

What else did the fair mean to us…?

Pitching pennies at cheap glass bowls. The world's biggest snake and the world's smallest horse – both for a dime. The smell of diesel fumes as a hundred generators ran the midway rides. The Esplanade lit up at night. Watching the WRR disc jockeys live at work. The Monorail and the Swiss Skyride. Big Tex shouting "Howdy Folks…". Sally Rand and her Revue, Arabian Horse Shows. First prize for the best pies. A twice daily circus and the Marine Marching Band. Horse shows and pig races. The Twister, The Wild Mouse and the Scrambler. The World Series of Rodeo. Gill Gray's Circus. The Texas Sports Hall of Fame.

A souvenir pillowcase, bought right on the Midway!

And that's not all folks...The Texas – OU Game. The Tilt-A-Whirl. Elsie the Cow and prize-winning hogs. Guess Your Weight. Mark Wilson's Magic Show. The State Fair Musicals. Bumper cars and the Dunk 'Em Booth. The Ice Capades. The Roll-O-Plane and The Hammer. Giant sunglasses and stuffed animal prizes. Paddle Boats. The Monkey Races and the Hum-A-Tune salesman who could make a thousand sounds with a little round hunk of plastic stuck in his mouth.

Step right up folks, there's even *more* to see and experience...The tiny "Mechanical City", The Swenson Thrillcade, Jack's French Fries, The Parisian Follies, The Cotton Bowl, The Automobile Building, The Swine Pavilion, The Women's Building, The Hall of State, Orange Julius, Cotton Candy, Salt Water Taffy, Fat Freddie the World's Biggest Human, throwing baseballs at lead-filled milk bottles. The Dancing Waters. And rides, rides, rides: The Cuddle Up, Fly-O-Plane, The Rotor, Flying Carousel, The Octopus, The Roundup, The Himalaya, The Matterhorn, The Paratrooper, The Carousel, The Calypso and The Ride-N-Laff.

Superstars

Celebrities performing at the Fair back in the day included Hopalong Cassidy, Elvis Presley, Homer and Jethro, George Gobel, Arthur Godfrey, Victor Borge, The McGuire Sisters, Jimmy Clanton, Chubby Checker, Mitch Miller, Fabian, Brenda Lee, Duane Eddy, Richard Rodgers, Lloyd Price, Kai Winding, Rex Allen, Bobby Vinton, Tennessee Ernie, Pat Boone, Candy Candido and Nelson Eddy.

51

The State Fair Musicals of the 50's
 South Pacific in 1950
 Guys and Dolls in 1951
 The Dean Martin and Jerry Lewis Revue in 1952
 The Ethel Merman Show in 1953
 The King and I in 1954
 Pajama Game in 1955
 Damn Yankees in 1956
 My Fair Lady in 1957
 The Music Man in 1958
 The McGuire Sister Revue in 1959
 Flower Drum Song in 1960

All of that's what The Great State Fair of Texas meant to me and to most of us who grew up in the 50's and 60's.

This is a photo of Elvis Presley performing in the center of the Cotton Bowl at the State Fair of Texas on October 11, 1956. Notice the hay-covered stage, a very Texas thing to do.

An ad for the 1956 State Fair on the day Elvis appeared.

Fast Facts
Around 14,000 people attend the opening day of the first fair back in 1886.

During World War I in 1918, they cancelled the fair as the fairgrounds were being used as US Army training camp.

Construction of the Cotton Bowl started in 1930 and the first Cotton Bowl Classic game was in 1937.

Big Tex made his debut in 1952.

Also in 1952, the Ride-N-Laff, one of the fair's most popular rides was installed on the Midway.

Elvis and the Monorail were big hits of the 1956 fair.

Richard Nixon showed up to cut the opening day ribbon in 1959.

The Swiss Skyride made its first appearance in 1964

The first big hill on the Comet Rollercoaster at Fair Park. Try and remember the clack-clack-clack as you slowly went up the hill. The moment of hesitation as the car reached the top. And the astonishingly fast drop to the bottom. The Comet roared from 1947 'til 1985.

Postcard from the fifties. Remember how you were told "if we get separated we'll meet at Big Tex"?

Teen Timers
The Music Scene in the 50s

Dallas was always a hoppin' music scene and in the fifties, with the advent of rock and roll and the boomers just becoming teenagers, the local musicians started boppin'.

The Atmospheres – This was Jack Allday's band prior to The Nightcaps. They had a local record called *The Fickle Chicken*. Also in the band: Bill Kramer, Clarke Brown, Steve Voekel and Ben Hill.

The Big Beats – A traditional 50s-sytle rock band with plaid jackets and bow-ties, they rocked pretty darn hard. They are credited with being the first rock band to sign with Columbia Records.

Tommy Brown and the Tom Toms – This was one of the ace bands in Dallas in the late 50s, the house band at The Guthrey Club. After Tommy Brown left, they backed up Gene Summers and then split off to become Sam The Sham and the Pharaohs.

Gaylon Christie and the Downbeats – Country and rock performers, they cut a string of local records and were big in the area nightclubs.

The Continentals – They recorded songs like *Kangaroo Hop* on the local Vandan label. Led by Bobby Charles.

Bobby Crown and the Kapers - In 1959 they recorded *One Way Ticket* and were a very popular club band.

—

Ronnie Dawson – He started as a rocker in the fifties, moved to banjo bands and folk singing in the sixties and back to hot rocking when his career took off again in the 90s.

Johnny Gee and the G-Men
An R&B flavored band which continued successfully into the sixties.

The Don Hosek Band – Formerly called The Jokers, they played dances and clubs. Jamie Bassett of the sixties band The Chaparrals says that in the late '50's Hosek's band was one of the most popular in town.

Don Hudson and the Royal Kings – Filled clubs all over town.

Jesse Lopez – With two different groups in the late fifties – The Knights and the Misters – Trini's brother was a sax player and singer who played on the Nightcaps' classic *Wine Wine Wine*. The Misters were a popular group from North Dallas High School.

Trini Lopez – Became famous after leaving for the coast but was a popular entertainer in area in the late 50s.

The Martels – Longtime Dallas band, made many club and TV appearances.

Scotty McKay – His real name was Max Lipscomb and he began his career as a back-up singer and guitarist with Gene Vincent. All told Scotty probably recorded 50 or more singles in the '50s, '60s and '70s. Even he couldn't remember them all.

—

Gene Summers – see listing below

<u>Buddy Miller and his Rockin' Ramblers</u> – A rockabilly outfit that could flat tear down the house. They had a local hit with *Little Bo Pete*.

<u>Vince Murphy & the Catalinas</u> – Club and dance rocking combo from Oak Cliff. He recorded a great rocker called *Speechless* way back in 1956.

The Nightcaps – With local super hits *Wine Wine Wine, 24 Hours* and *Thunderbird,* these guys were the hottest thing in town in the late '50s and early '60s. Billy Joe Shine was the vocalist, Mario Daboub was the leader and bassist, Jack Allday was on drums, Gene Haufler on rhythm guitar and David Swartz played the lead guitar. They influenced every young player in town from Denny Freeman to Jimmie and Stevie Ray Vaughan.

Bobby Poe and the Poe Kats – A top local bar band and hot rockabillies.

Gene Rambo and the Flames – From high school dances to recording studios around town, Gene and the Flames were serious rockers.

Bobby Rambo – With and without his brother Gene, Bobby Rambo was a great guitarist who was with several successful local bands through the sixties (The In Crowd, Jimmy Rabbit's band, even The Five Americans for a while.)

The Straightjackets (with Delbert McClinton) – This Fort Worth band played all over the area and backed up Bruce Channel on the national hit *Hey Baby*.

Kirby St. Romain – Hit in the early 60s with with *Summer's Coming*.

Gene Summers and the Rebels – The local hits kept coming for Gene from *Straight Skirts* through *Big Blue Diamond*s.

Ray Sharpe – Fort Worth blues rocker had a national hit with *Linda Lu* in 1959.

Jimmy Velvit – Local blues-crooner who immortalized the song *(You're Mine) We Belong Together* for a generation of North Texas kids.

Joe Wilson and the Sabres – Another well-known hot local club band.

**Other Local
Musical Notes:**
On September 3, 1955, if you had only known, you could have seen Elvis Presley perform live at a Dallas nightclub called The Round Up. The cover charge was a buck.

In 1957 Dallas musician Scotty McKay performed on the Ed Sullivan show as a guitarist with Gene Vincent and the Blue Caps (Scotty is shown second from the left in the photo below.)

For The Record

During the fifties, the recording industry in Dallas blossomed. Recording in local metroplex studios were such nationally known country music performers as Lefty Frizzell, Marty Robbins, Ray Price and Johnny Horton. Each of these internationally famous acts recorded at Jim Beck's legendary studio in Dallas. As did Dallas rockabilly legend Lew Williams.

Roy Orbison's first recording session took place in Dallas in December of 1955 at Jim Beck's Studio. Accompanied by his band The Teen Kings, Orbison recorded the demo for his first hit *Ooby Dooby*.

At Seller's Recording Studio in downtown and at the Top Ten Studios on Ross Avenue, such varied acts as Gene Vincent, Esquerita, Johnny Carroll, George Jones, Whistlin' Alex Moore, Gene Summers and "Groovey" Joe Poovey recorded during the fifties.

Fort Worth singer and songwriter Ray Sharpe enjoyed national success with his record *Linda Lu* in 1959.

Blues artists also were drawn to Dallas to record in the fifties. In DFW area studios were ZuZu Bollin, Lloyd Fulson and others.

Vince Murphy and the Catalinas — late 50's

In 1960 superstar Conway Twitty and Scotty McKay headlined the KBOX New Year's Eve show for teenagers. Held at Memorial Auditorium, it was (supposedly) an alcohol-free event. Four hours of rockin' fun for $1.50. Not too bad. Happy New Year!

Kat's Karavan. Starting in the fifties WRR 1310 presented a weekly show featuring rhythm and blues music. Hosted by Jim Lowe, the program was one of the first in Texas to feature primarily blues and r&b music aimed at a primarily white teenage audience. "Kat's Karavan" dared to play the music that other white radio stations in

Dallas shied away from. Blues legends like Jimmy Reed, T-Bone Walker and Muddy Waters were given prominent airtime, broadening their appeal to white teens in the area.

Due to their exposure on the show the local band The Nightcaps became Dallas' number one band. Their hit "Wine, Wine, Wine" is still remembered as one of the most rockin' songs of the late fifties.

Longhorn Ballroom

In 1950 Dewey Groom opened The Longhorn Ballroom at Corinth and Industrial. For over 50 years, this huge dance club has featured almost every type of musical performer, from The Light Crust Doughboys to The Sex Pistols.

Sounds Like The Fifties

In Dallas KLIF and KGKO (later known as KBOX) played the Top 40 rock 'n' roll songs we loved. Here is a list of the top selling rock-style songs from 1955 – 1960*

> (only one song per artist listed)
>
> *Rock Around The Clock* – Bill Haley and his Comets
> *Hound Dog* – Elvis Presley
> *Maybelline* – Chuck Berry
> *Honky Tonk* – Bill Doggett
> *Little Darlin'* – The Diamonds
> *All I Have To Do Is Dream* – The Everly Brothers
> *Tequila* – The Champs
> *At The Hop* – Danny and the Juniors
> *Personality* – Lloyd Price
> *The Twist* – Chubby Checker

* Source: Cashbox Magazine

Local Television in the 50's

Over in Fort Worth WBAP-TV Channel 5 became the first TV station in our area, signing on September 29, 1948 affiliated with the national NBC-TV Network. It was followed quickly by KBTS, later known as WFAA (Channel 8) and KRLD (CBS Channel 4). The independent Channel 11 (then KFJZ) signed on in 1955.

From the start the programs were a bit spotty. Programs along the lines of local book review shows, cooking programs, old western movies and news dominated the earliest days. Viewers by the millions (OK – hundreds. Dozens?) tuned into WBAP for shows like "Gardening Can Be Fun" and "What's New Ladies?".

TV Sets were not inexpensive in the early days. A set
in 1952 could cost 10% of a family's annual income.

Movies were a staple of local TV literally from the first day. WBAP aired "The Scarlet Pimpernel" starring Leslie Howard on that September 29 broadcast. Within a couple of years several regular wild western movie presentations were on local TV like *Frontier Roundup, Frontier Playhouse, Cowboy Classics,* and *Cowboy Thrills.* Old "b" westerns were plentiful and cheap, so rarely did a day go by without at least one appearing on one of the three local channels.

The very first live, local entertainment show was a country-music classic called "The Flying X Ranch Boys" also on WBAP. The boys were a spin-off of the Light Crust Doughboys. Channel 5 kept up its C&W beginnings in the early days with shows like *Barn Dance* on Saturday nights. By the start of 1950 there were close to 20,000 TV sets in the DFW area, a number which grew rapidly each year.

On September 17, 1949 KBTV Channel 8 signed on as an affiliate of the DuMont Television Network. The station was the first in Dallas and the second in the TV market area. The next March the station ownership changed hands and it became WFAA-TV. When the DuMont Network shut down in 1955, WFAA became the area's ABC affiliate.

CBS affiliate KRLD-TV began broadcasting on December 3, 1949, owned by The Dallas Times Herald.

Other very early local shows included *Sportatorium Wrestling, The Julie Benell Show, Bob Stanford's Preview, Over the Coffee Cups, Parade of Champions, What's Cooking?* and *News Roundup.*

Hey Bud, Whatcha Lookin' At?

Remember these two little guys? The one on the right would kick the other and ask "Hey bud, whatcha lookin' at?" After getting no response he would kick again and ask more emphatically "Hey bud, whatcha lookin' at?" To which the guy on the left would simply reply "Channel 11." The one on the right would then add the capper: "Umm, umm. Good Lookin'".

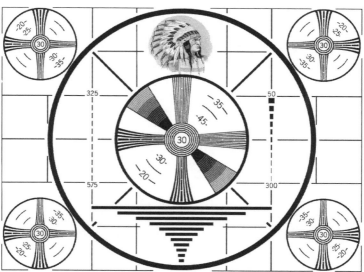

At an early age we learned that if you stared at the Indian long enough, Cartoon Clubhouse would come on.

Local TV Musical Memories

"Foremost Teen Times" aired on WBAP-TV in Fort Worth, in 1954 starring Pat Boone. Yes, THAT Pat Boone who was a student at North Texas State University at the time.

In 1958 Jerry Haynes began to host "Dallas Bandstand" on Channel 8. It was a local version of "American Bandstand" with local teen dancers participating in the program. Haynes eventually got the chance to substitute for Dick Clark on the national version of the show.

Left: News, weather and sports on Channel 4 included future Dallas mayor Wes Wise. On the right, Channel 8 funny man Big Don Norman hosted movie shows featuring skits and satirical comments.

The Big D Jamboree

Beginning in the late forties, and finding its largest audience in the mid-fifties, *The Big D Jamboree* became Dallas' number one country music show. Broadcast live over KRLD radio every Saturday night, the show originated from Ed McLemore's Sportatorium at 1000 South Industrial.

In its earliest days the show was a lower budget Texas version of "The Grand Old Opry", with traditional country and hillbilly acts featured. Beginning in the mid-fifties, the Sportatorium stage began to showcase the stars of the early days of rock and roll and rockabilly.

Each Saturday night, many national and local musical acts took the stage to play for packed houses of up to 5000 fans per show. Among the top national acts who performed were Hank Williams, Sonny James, Lefty Frizzell, Hank Snow, Johnny Cash, Carl Perkins and at the beginning of his career, Elvis Presley.

Talented local performers were often the highlights of the shows, and such acts as Sid King and the Five Stings, "Groovey" Joe Poovey, Johnny Carroll, The Belew Twins and Ronnie Dawson performed regularly.

In its later days, The Jamboree was also featured on local television, giving fans who could not attend in person the opportunity to see their favorite performers.

From 1948 until the mid-sixties *The Big D Jamboree* was a Dallas entertainment tradition.

Above: Carl "Blue Suede Shoes" Perkins performs at The Big D Jamboree. Left to right: Clayton Perkins, Fluke Holland, Carl Perkins and Jay Perkins. Lower: Charline Arthur and her band pose outside the Sportatorium.

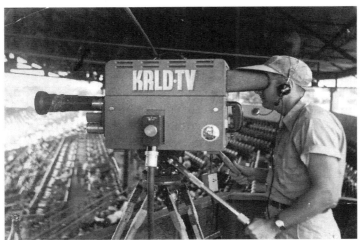

Live sporting events were a fixture of local TV from the earliest days. Here a Channel 4 cameraman catches the action.

On Channel 8, Bob Stanford hosted a local game and entertainment show called "Dollar Derby".

Television Log Thursday

N (NBC); D (DuMont); A (ABC); C (CBS)

Dallas— A.M.	WFAA-TV Channel 8	KRLD-TV Dallas— Channel 4	WBAP-TV Fort Worth— Channel 5
6:00	Today: Dave Garroway N	Morning Show C	Sunup C
6:15	" " ; Dallas Today	" Agriculture	
6:30	" "	"	
6:45	" " ; Dallas Today	"	Breakfast Club A
7:00	" "	"	
7:15	" ; Dallas Today	" Weather	
7:30	" "	"	
7:45	" ; Dallas Today	" Local News	
8:00	Maggie and Her Friends;	Garry Moore C	Ding Dong
8:15	Magic Forest Stories	"	School N
8:30	Summer School;	Arthur Godfrey C	A Time to Live N
8:45	Ben Show	"	3 Steps to Heaven N
9:00	Money Man	"	Home: With
9:15	" "; Devotionals	"	Arlene Francis N
9:30	"	Strike It Rich C	"
9:45	Cozy Corner	"	"
10:00	Betty White Show;	Valiant Lady C	Movie Marquee:
10:15	Musical Revue N	Love of Life C	"In the Money"
10:30	The Ruggles;	Search for Tomorrow C	Sheets Gallagher
10:45	Charlie Ruggles	Guiding Light C	Sally Starr
11:00	Julie Benell, Recipes	Beauty Show C	Musical Memo
11:15	From Food Editor of	Cartoons; News C	"; Pastor
11:30	Dallas Morning News	Welcome Traveler C	Diane Lucas
11:45			Show
Noon	The Money Man Show:	Featurette	Farm Editor
12:15	Bob King, Emcee	Robert Q. Lewis C	Weather; News
12:30	Claire Stewart, Ray Plagens	House Party C	Buddy Peters
12:45	Noon Edition	"	Show
1:00	Showtime Matinee:	The Big Payoff C	Greatest Gift N
1:15	"Study in Charcoal"	"	Golden Windows N
1:30	Guest Book: Jerry Haynes,	Bob Crosby C	One Man's Family N
1:45	Joan Oliver, Ray Plagens	"	Miss Marlowe N
2:00	Hawkins Falls	Brighter Day C	What's Cooking
2:15	First Love	Secret Storm C	(Colorcast)
2:30	Bob Smith Show:	On Your	"
2:45	With Skitch Henderson N	Account C	"
3:00	Duchess Playhouse:	Mary Carter	Movie Marquee:
3:15	"Come to the Book"	Cook Book	"Return of
3:30	Howdy Doody	Portia Faces Life C	Rin-Tin-Tin"
3:45	of Doodyville, U.S.A.	Variety Fair	Bobby Blake
4:00	Kiddie Karnival		Ann Alden
4:15	With Miss Ben	Martha McDonald's	Six-Gun Theater
4:30	Frontier Playhouse	Kitchen	"
4:45	with Alvarado		"
5:00	Time for Magic	Party Time	See Saw Zoo
5:15	John Daly and the News A	"	"
5:30	Vaughn Monroe Show	Douglas Edwards N	Cartoon Time
5:45	NewsCaravan:JohnSwayze N	Jane Froman C	World, Local News
6:00	Evening Edition	Flash Gordon	Cowboy Thrills
6:15	Baseball Hall of Fame	"	"; Weather
6:30	Melody Tour: Musical	Four Star	Lone Ranger A
6:45	Variety Revue	Playhouse C	"
7:00	Football in the News	What Do You Have	Dragnet N
7:15	With Bill Rives	In Common?	"
7:30	Name's the Same: Robert	Big Town	Theater C
7:45	Q. Lewis, Quizmaster A	"	"
8:00	So You Want to Lead	Talltale Clue C	Video Theater N
8:15	a Band: Sammy Kaye A	"	"
8:30	Captured;	Name That Tune C	"
8:45	Chester Morris	"	"
9:00	Boston Blackie:	Kiwanis Auction	Justice N
9:15	Kent Taylor	"	"
9:30	Dangerous Assignment:	"	You Bet Your Life:
9:45	Starring Brian Donlevy	"	Groucho Marx N
10:00	Final Edition	World Today	Texas News
10:15	Mystery Playhouse:	Weather; Sports	Weather; News
10:30	"Tananga"—Mona Knox	Kiwanis Auction	Sports; Movie:
10:45	Channel 8 Theater:	"	"Rimfire," Mary
11:00	"Girl From Manhattan"	"	Beth Hughes,
11:15	Starring Dorothy Lamour	"	James Millican,
11:30	And Charles Laughton	"	Henry Hull
11:45	(To Midnight)	(To Midnight)	(To Midnight)

Television Log Saturday

N (NBC); A (ABC); C (CBS)

Channel 8 WFAA-TV A.M. The Dallas News	Channel 4 KRLD-TV Dallas	Channel 5 WBAP-TV Fort Worth	CHOICE
7:00			CHOICE
7:15			ON
7:30			CHANNEL 8
7:45 Farm Parade	Sign On (7.58)		
8:00 Farm Parade	Cartoon		Classic
8:15 Cowboy Classics:	Time		
8:30 "Pals of the	Captain	Let's Teach	Rivals
8:45 Range," R. Lease	Kangaroo	Kangaroo	
9:00 Hans Christian	"	Howdy Doody	USC
9:15 Anderson	"	Show N	
9:30 I Married Joan:	Johnny	Captain	and
9:45 Joan Davis B	Jupiter	Midnight	
10:00 His Honor,	Winky Dink	Fury N	UCLA
10:15 Homer Bell	and You C	"	
10:30 Uncle Johnny	Texas Rangers C	Bobby Peters	Clash
10:45 Coons	"	Jamboree	
11:00 Cowboy Theater:	Mighty Mouse C	Twin Fairies	at
11:15 Charles Starrett	"	Six Gun	
11:30 "	Buffalo Bill	Theater	3:15 p.m.
11:45	"	"	

P.M. Channel 8	Channel 4	Channel 5	Channel 11 KFJZ-TV Fort Worth
Noon Western	The Lone	Farm Editor	
12:15 Marshal	Ranger C	"	Saturday
12:30 Jungle Jim: "Men	Sky King		Matinee Public Service
12:45 from Xanzibar"	"	Saturday	
1:00 Whip Wilson	Backstage	Matinee	Cartoon Hour
1:15 "Riders of		"Riding the	
1:30 the Dusk"	College Football	Dusty Trail";	Theater 11:
1:45	Roundup	"Affairs of	"Riding the
2:00 Saturday	With	Cappy Ricks"	California
2:15 Playhouse:	Scenes		Trail,"
2:30 "Fighting Back,"	From	Game of	Gilbert Roland
2:45 Paul Langdon	Over	the Week	; News
3:00 NCAA Preview	the	Forecast	
3:15 NCAA Football	Nation	Preview	Jalopy
3:30 Game of	"	NCAA Football	Derby
3:45 the week:	"	Game of	Dude Ranchers
4:00 UCLA	"	the Week:	Western
4:15 vs.	"	UCLA	Theater
4:30 USC,	Questions	vs.	"
4:45 Lindsey Nelson	Featurette	USC,	"
5:00 and	Big B Jamboree	Lindsey	Continental
5:15 Red Grange	"	Nelson,	Teen Club
5:30	Cartoon Time	Red Grange N	"
5:45	Football Final	"	"

P.M. Channel 8	Channel 4	Channel 5	Channel 11
6:00 Stars of Grand	Beat the	NCAA Scores N	Dutch Meyer
6:15 Old Opry	Clock	This Is Story	on Football
6:30 People Are Funny:	The Buccaneers	"	News, Sports
6:45 Art Linkletter N	"	I Spy	; Weather
7:00 Man Called X;	Jackie Gleason	Perry Como	Top Plays
7:15 Barry Sullivan	Show C	Show N	of '56
7:30 Frontier:	"	"	Conference
7:45 "Out of Taos"	"	"	Table
8:00 Lawrence Welk	Gale Storm	Saturday Night Movie:	
8:15 Show:	Show C	Spectacular:	The Long
8:30 Alice Lon,	Roy Jeannie C	"High Button	Search,"
8:45 Larry Dean A	"	Shoes,"	George Nader,
9:00 Masquerade	Gunsmoke C	Nat March,	Anita Hart
9:15 Party A	"	Don Ameche	
9:30 Science Fiction	High Finance C	(Colorcast) N	News; Weather
9:45 Theater	"	"	Saturday
10:00 National Pro	Fabian of	Texas News	Night
10:15 Highlights	Scotland Yard	Weather; News	Fights
10:30 Final News	Eddy Arnold	Scores; LesPaul	Sports; Movie:
10:45 Final Sports	"	Movie:	"Rapture,"
11:00 United Artists	Wrestling	"The Body	Hugo
11:15 Hour: No Man	"	Snatcher,"	Langan,
11:30 All the Way,	"	Boris Karloff,	Eloy
11:45 John Garfield	"	Bela Lugosi	Albin
Mdnt.	Midnight (to 1)	Sign Off	Sign Off

On the left – here's what you could see on an average Thursday night in 1954. In the morning we liked *Maggie and Her Friends* and *Ding Dong School*. *Kiddie Karnival* came on at 4PM followed by action westerns on *Frontier Playhouse*. Mark Wilson's local show *Time For Magic* followed that. On the right is a typical Saturday line-up in the fall of 1956. The kid show classics included *Johnny Jupiter*, *Sky King*, *Captain Kangaroo*, *Captain Midnight* and *Winky Dink*.

75

Twerps in Wonderland
The Local Kid Shows
Of The 50's

Before there was an Icky Twerp there was a lot of Dallas kid-show territory. Cowboys introducing western movies. Ladies reading wonderful stories. And a couple of Captains.

When I was about five years old, I received a shock that has stayed with me to this day. The event taught me a valuable lesson, however, and that was simply "Hey kid, don't believe everything you see."

In 1954 or so, there was a popular kid show on WFAA, Channel 8. If memory serves it was called "Captain Bob's Kiddie Karnival." Along with Captain Bob were his electronic sidekick "Mickey The Microphone" and other critters.

When my friends and I had the chance to be a part of the live studio kid audience, we were all excited. My friends wanted to see the inside of a real television studio.

Personally, I wanted to see one particular performer on the show, who I remember being called "Timmy The Bear", my favorite TV "personality". Up close and in person. Timmy was as tall as the Captain, a big furry yet friendly creature. As bears go, he was cooler than Smokey and less threatening than the one that Davy Crockett wrestled.

There was just one problem with Timmy The Bear. He wasn't a bear. He was a guy in a bear suit. I discovered this to my horror after Timmy stepped offstage away from the hot lights, behind the cameras, and removed his fake bear head in an attempt to find some relief from the heat.

——

CAP'N BOB'S KIDDIE KARNIVAL
The reading of the birthday book is a daily feature of Channel 8's children's show, Kiddie Karnival, which celebrates its own first birthday Monday. Starring Cap'n Bob, who is really Bob Blase, the show will be seen on WFAA-TV each weekday afternoon at a new time, 5 p.m., beginning Monday.

After hearing his cue he popped the head back on and trotted out onto the stage again, bouncing and dancing.

Timmy, say it ain't so! You're a guy in a bear suit? Bouncing and dancing and fooling the kids of Dallas in your fake costume? I was crushed. Timmy The Bear lost his head and his credibility in one fell swoop.

MORE KID STUFF – Early 50's

By the early 50's, the boomers began paying attention to the local kid shows and regular cartoon shows. WBAP led the way in Saturday morning kid shows too. By 1953 their line up included *Bobby Peters Jamboree, Sky King, Space Patrol* and *Laugh Time.*

Another local kid show on Channel 5 was *Tricks or Treats* and starred local cartoonist Johnny Hay, assisted by magician "Mr. Mystic". Mystic provided the magic tricks and Hay drew cartoon treats for the kiddies. Ah, times really were simpler back in 1950 weren't they?

Channel 8 also featured Ben January as "Alvarado" - the host of a series of western movies, and Miss Bea - the hostess of *Kiddie Karnival.* "Maggie and her friends" brought us early morning stories on *Magic Forest Stories,* also on WFAA.

Above: Live TV on WBAP in 1954

Another favorite TV kids' program was local afternoon show on Channel 8 featured "cowboy hero" The Frito Kid played by Bob Stanford. In the short filmed show, invariably our hero, The Kid, was called on to save the lovely Lulubelle from the clutches of that nasty sidewinder Snakebit Sam (played by Agnes Stanford and Easy Marvin respectively.)

This Guy Quacks Me Up

We can't forget the classic Channel 8 show featuring the duck puppet known as Webster Webfoot. The afternoon program was sponsored by Sanger Brothers department store. Along with his human companion Jimmy Weldon, the pair became very popular with the kids, and eventually moved on to Los Angeles for a long and successful TV career.

Wilson's 'Time for Magic' In Channel 8 Debut Today

Time for Magic, a show designed especially for children, will debut on WFAA-TV, Tuesday at 5:30 p.m. with Magician Mark Wilson as star.

The quarter-hour show, to be sponsored by tne Dr. Pepper Company, will be seen on Channel 8 each Tuesday and Thursday afternoon, and will feature Wilson in an array of slight-of-hand feats.

Children of the Dallas-Fort Worth area will be invited to help Wilson perform his tricks on the new TV show providing they qualify for membership in his Magic Club.

Wilson, a graduate of Southern Methodist University, is a professional entertainer, and has been a magic enthusiast since the age of eight. He is well known regionally after having made more than 400 appearances at the State Fair of Texas during the last four years.

Above: Mark Wilson, Nani Darnell and Rebo The Clown hosted a local TV magic show. (The magic word was "Dr. Pepper". Can ya guess who the sponsor was?) Mark Wilson went on to national fame with the network TV show "The Magic Land of Alakazam".

Also on Channel 5 was the first local "story lady" – former Hollywood Starlet Mary 'Punkins' Parker, (above) who sat and read stories to her entranced young audience on *Mary Parker Playtime*. Later Kitty Atkins would fill this role in WBAP's fondly remembered cartoon-and-live-story show *Kitty's Wonderland*.

Kitty's Wonderland . . . . .
WBAP-TV Success Story

The star of "Kitty's Wonderland," the highest rated daytime TV show in all the Fort Worth-Dallas area in 1957, is a 1950 graduate of Hardin-Simmons University.

In private life Kitty is the wife of Luther Adkins who serves as WBAP's Public Service and Religious Coordinator. Luther says he is a Hardin-Simmons University graduate by marriage.

Kitty is the former Kathleen Ritter from Anson. She received her B. A. degree in 1950 with a major in Sociology and a minor in Bible. Here on the campus she was in the Life Service Band, Y. W. A., and the Anson Club. In 1949 she was University Beauty and in 1950 she was elected to Who's Who.

After graduation she spent six years working for the Home Mission Board of the Southern Baptist Convention doing the thing at which she is most adept—telling stories to children.

"Kitty's Wonderland" was first presented on WBAP-TV April 25, 1955. The hour long program is presented Monday through Friday from 8:00 to 9:00 A. M. It is primarily designed to appeal to tots from 2 to 6 years old. However, numerous children up to 16 years of age watch the "Wonderland".

The show consists of five different parts. To start off, film cartoons by Walter Lantz are shown. Next is stories read by Kitty, with Bible stories each Friday. After the stories birthdays are acknowledged.

(Continued on Page 15)

Pictured below in the studios of WBAP-TV is Mrs. Luther Adkins, star of Kitty's Wonderland. While on the H-SU campus she was Kitty Ritter and graduated in 1950 with a B. A. degree.

KITTY'S WONDERLAND . . . .

(Continued from Page 6)

Then verses submitted by boys and girls are read. All of this is climaxed by a helpful hint each day.

To prove how successful the show is, all you have to do is look at the stacks of mail that comes in each week. The first 90 days the show was on the air, a total of 5,724 letters were received. The all time high was reached between July 7, and July 15, 1956, when Kitty's mail reached the staggering figure of 22,-000 pieces.

Mothers have expressed their gratitude to "Kitty's Wonderland" for its entertainment value. The show has been dubbed a "TV Baby Sitter."

Personable, pretty and young Kitty has a 3 year old daughter of her own, so she understands children and takes delight in entertaining them. Her popularity in the Fort Worth-Dallas area is unquestioned.

Kitty would read wonderful stories to us in a quiet, reassuring voice. I remember that when the show would begin each day, a neighbor's mom would ring a bell signaling to the kids playing outside to come in for *Kitty's Wonderland.*

82

Mickey Mudturtle and Amanda Possum were such local stars in the mid-fifties that they could bring a thousand kids to a shopping center opening in Farmers Branch.

In 1955, KFJZ-TV Channel 11 signed on with a strong emphasis on movies and filmed syndicated programs. But like most local channels, they also produced their own programs and kid shows were easy and cheap to do.

On KFJZ, Channel 11, George Nolan was Cap'n Swabby introducing Popeye cartoons. "Cartoon Alley" with Albert the Alley Cat and starring Miss Lynn was a fixture in the late '50s.

Some of Channel 11's other shows aimed at kids included The Gene Autry Show, Cartoon Clubhouse, Range Rider, The Little Rascals, Ramar of the Jungle, Terry and the Pirates, The Roy Rogers Show and Porky's Playhouse.

Ramar of the Jungle, one of the syndicated shows aimed at kids which Channel 11 ran in the pre-primetime afternoons in 1956. The series starred Jon Hall as Ramar.

Dean Allen Stars As 'Friendly' On Channel 4

Dean Allen, the original voice of Donald Duck, has been signed to take over as emcee of the "Uncle Tiny" show on KRLD-TV, Channel 4, replacing the late Tiny Grant.

The new show which will be called "Officer Friendly" with Allen portraying a kindly policeman who is a friend of young children will start Monday in the old spot from 5 to 6 p.m.

Allen has secured permission from Walt Disney to feature the Donald Duck voice and character on his show.

Allen got his start in show business in Dallas as a featured entertainer with the old Interstate Theaters shows.

Who could forget Dean Allen as "Officer Friendly"? The name stuck in our minds and soon every rent-a-cop at every dance in town was referred to as Officer Friendly. His puppet was known as Jimmy Duck and using his catch phrase "Jimmy Duck go waddle-waddle" was an irritating local fad in the early sixties.

The Twerp Years

Slam Bang Theater a local kid show starring Bill Camfield as "Icky Twerp" premiered on Channel 11 in the mid-fifties. Icky's "gorilla" sidekicks named "Delphinium, Ajax and Arkadelphia" became almost as well known as the host. These were three performers who really earned the titles of "Second Bananas".

Bill Camfield as Icky Twerp and Ajax and Delphinium

86

Bill Camfield was born in 1929 in Mineral Wells just west of Fort Worth. He and his mother moved to Fort Worth when he was young, and after graduating from high school, he became a copywriter in the ad department of Leonard's Department Stores. This led to a Leonard's sponsored TV show called "Hometown Harmony" which Bill hosted.

When Channel 11 (then KFJZ) signed on in 1954, Bill went to work there as a copywriter, program creator and jack of all trades. Although he appeared in news shows, other kids' shows and on commercials, we will always remember him best as either Icky Twerp on *Slam Bang Theater* or as "Gorgon" the spooky host of *Nightmare*, the Channel 11 movie show specializing in horror and science fiction thrillers.

As Icky Twerp he threw and received pies, interacted with stage-hands wearing ape masks (Ajax, Delphinium and later Arkadephia). To get the Three Stooges short subjects rolling, Icky would climb on a bizarre bike-pedal controlled "movie machine", pedal away and the Stooges would start.

One of the things we liked best on *Slam Bang Theater* about Icky Twerp and his cohorts is that they weren't always...*nice*. They hit people with pies. They knocked stuff over. They pulled chairs out from under each other. They threw food, splashed other people with paint and stuff and when they got mad, they threw tantrums. Unlike all the polite, sweet-natured TV hosts (Mr. Peppermint, Miss Mary Ann on Romper Room and so on) Icky and his nutty pals were more like real kids. We liked that nice Miss Kitty on *Kitty's Wonderland*, but we idolized Icky Twerp. He was one of us.

Slam Bang Theater left Channel 11 in the late 60's and by then most of us had moved on, too. We left him behind, but we never forgot Icky Twerp.

———

National TV Shows We Loved

Dale Evans and Roy Rogers

Happy Trails - Cowboy Heroes of National TV

The Roy Rogers Show
Tales of the Texas Rangers
Annie Oakley
The Gene Autry Show
Hopalong Cassidy
The Lone Ranger
Rin Tin Tin
Maverick
Cheyenne
Sugarfoot
Have Gun, Will Travel
Wild Bill Hickock
The Cisco Kid
Range Rider
Sergeant Preston of the Yukon
Rin Tin Tin
Sky King

50's Kid Shows

Captain Gallant
Captain Kangaroo
Captain Midnight
Captain Video
Circus Boy
Commando Cody
Ding Dong School
Fearless Fosdick
Fury
Howdy Doody
Jungle Jim
Kukla, Fran and Ollie
Lassie
The Magic Land of Alakazam
The Mickey Mouse Club
Mr. I. Magination
Mr. Wizard
Pinky Lee
Ramar of the Jungle
Rocky Jones, Space Ranger
Rootie Kazootie
Sheena Queen of the Jungle
Soupy Sales
Space Patrol
Super Circus
Superman
Tom Corbett, Space Cadet
Winchell and Mahoney
Winky Dink

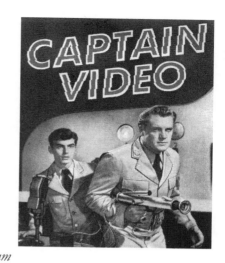

George Reeves as *Superman*

DING DONG SCHOOL

Miss Frances, the beloved, grandmotherly lady who taught us that we could be nice, behave and still have fun.

"Hey Kids, What Time Is It?

It's *Howdy Doody* Time!

Buffalo Bob Smith created and hosted this fondly remembered show which ran from 1947 to 1960. A studio audience of kids sat in 'The Peanut Gallery' as they were entertained by puppets Howdy, his twin brother Double Doody, Mr. Bluster, Dilly Dally, The Flubadub, John J. Fadoozle ("America's #1 'boi-oing' Private Eye.") and humans like Chief Thunderthud ("Cowabunga!"), Princess SummerFallWinterSpring, J. Cornelius "Corny" Cobb and Clarabell the Clown.

*Left to Right Above: Phineas T. Bluster, Chief
Thunderthud and The Flubadub. Below: Judy
Tyler as Princess SummerFallWinterSpring - all from
The Howdy Doody Show*

The Mickey Mouse Club

Every weekday on Channel 8 in the mid-fifties, we were glued to the tube for our favorite national show, which actually starred kids our own age! With dancing, singing, skits, comedy and those heart-warming serials, for The Mickey Mouse Club was the entertainment event of each day. "Forever let us hold our banners high! M-I-C-K-E-Y M-O-U-S-E."

The Mickey Mouse Club Serials

Above left: Spin and Marty. Right: The Hardy Boys

The Adventures of Spin and Marty
Annette
The Boys of The Western Sea
Corky and White Shadow
The Hardy Boys Mysteries

OK, kids...sing along:

The theme song from *Spin and Marty*:
"When tenderfeet come to the Triple R, Yippee Yay Yippee
Yo! They get on a horse but they don't go far, Yippee Yay
Yippee Yo!"

The theme song from *The Hardy Boys:*
"Gold doubloons and pieces of eight,
Handed down to Applegate,
From buccaneers, who fought for years,
For Gold Doubloons, and Pieces of Eight..."

The Little Rascals

Channel 11 ran all sorts of wonderful short subjects from the 1930s and 1940's, most aimed at us kids. In addition to the Three Stooges on Slam Bang Theater, The Little Rascals were a morning favorite of ours.

In the afternoons, to fill time between movies and shows, the station ran comedy short subjects that both kids and their parents could enjoy. That's how we discovered the joys of almost forgotten 30's funnymen like Charlie Chase, Edgar Kennedy and Andy Clyde.

Above you see Darla serving a glass of 1¢ lemonade to Buckwheat, while Waldo, Alfalfa and Spanky look on. Partially obscured by the dipper is young Mickey Gubitosi, who grew up to be Emmy Award winning actor Robert Blake.

Beany and Cecil (featuring bad-guy Dishonest John)
Clutch Cargo (with Spinner and Paddlefoot)
Crusader Rabbit
Deputy Dawg
The Flintstones
George of the Jungle
Huckleberry Hound
The Jetsons
King Leonardo
The Mighty Hercules
Mighty Mouse
Quick Draw McGraw
Rocky and Bullwinkle
Ruff 'n' Reddy
Snagglepuss
Top Cat
Wally Gator
Woody Woodpecker
Yogi Bear

And don't forget: Augie Doggie and Doggie Daddy, Magilla Gorilla, Touche Turtle, Atom Ant, Jonny Quest, Secret Squirrel, Pixie and Dixie and Yacky Doodle.

Above: Beany and Cecil the Sea-Sick Sea Serpent

Andy's Gang

"Hiya kids...hiya hiya!" It's Froggy the Gremlin who would appear in a puff of smoke and a "boi-oi-oing" whenever Andy Devine said "Plunk your magic twanger, Froggy!"

Andy was the host of this fun show which aired on Saturday mornings at 9:30-10:00 am on Channel 5 from mid 1955 until the end of 1960.

The show also featured a violin playing cat named Midnight and filmed episodes of an adventure serial starring Gunga Ram the Jungle Boy. Introducing the show was Buster Brown (and his dog Tige) whose line of shoes just happened to sponsor the show.

———

King of the Wild Marketeers

The Adventures of Davy Crockett was a runaway hit in 1955 helping to put the young ABC Network on the ratings map. It was a five part series running in one hour episodes, the first three in 1955 and the final two the next year.

Fess Parker as The King of the Wild Frontier

$100 million dollars of Davy Crockett merchandise was sold nationwide in 1955 alone. Every kid – boy or girl – wanted a coonskin cap. There were also lunch boxes, collectors cards, Ol' Betsy cap rifles, play sets, books, comics, lamps, clothing and almost anything else you could imagine. Dallas area stores had difficulty keeping many of the items in stock. Not to mention the #1 hit song "The Ballad of Davy Crockett". Christmas of 1955 was Davy's year to make the big bucks.

The Lone Ranger

"A fiery horse with the speed of light, a cloud of dust and a hearty 'Hi-Yo Silver' – The Lone Ranger. With his loyal Indian companion Tonto, the daring and resourceful masked rider of the plains led the fight for law and order in the early west. Return with us now to those thrilling days of yesteryear. The Lone Ranger Rides Again!" Above Clayton Moore and Jay Silverheels as the Lone Ranger and Tonto.

So goodbye from Kid Show Land....

From Gumby and his horse Pokey

Remembered Prime Time Series

The Adventures of Ozzie and Harriett (1952 – 1966)
When the show began, Dave and Rick were pre-teens, but as they grew up, so did the story lines. Both teen actors became famous, and Ricky became one of the biggest teen idols of all time.

Father Knows Best (1954 - 1960)

Starred former matinee idol Robert Young. Elinor Donahue ("Princess") and Billy Gray ("Bud") and Lauren Chapin ("Kitten")

Leave It To Beaver (1957 – 1963)

Family sitcom in which the kids were the focus. Tony Dow and "Jerry Mathers as the Beaver" pictured below with Mom – Barbara Billingsley.

The Many Loves of Dobie Gillis (1959 – 1963)
Considered edgy and off-the-wall for the era, it was a huge comedy success.

Dwayne Hickman – Dobie Gillis
Bob Denver – Maynard G. Krebs
Tuesday Weld – Thalia Menninger
Warren Beatty – Milton Armitage

Above: Dwayne Hickman as Dobie and Bob Denver as Maynard G. Krebs. Maynard said the "G" stood for "Walter".

The Andy Griffith Show: Beloved, folksy show, one of the few from the era still in constant reruns. Andy Griffith, Ronny Howard, Don Knotts and Jim Nabors as Gomer Pyle.

My Three Sons (1960 – 1972)
There were actually four sons on this show and they were Tim Considine, Don Grady, Stanley Livingston and Barry Livingston. The latter two were real-life brothers.

Our Miss Brooks (1952 – 1956)
Although it was a comedy about the life of a high school teacher, it was often her students who stole the show. The main breakout actor was Richard Crenna who, although well out of his teens at the time, found stardom as nerdy Walter Denton.

The Donna Reed Show (1958 – 1966)
Although named for its star, the show often focused on the two teen kids, Shelley Fabares as Mary Stone and Paul Peterson as Jeff Stone

The Bob Cummings Show (1955 – 1959)
Bob Cummings starred as big-time Hollywood glamour photographer Bob Collins. With Dwayne Hickman as Chuck, Rosemary DeCamp as Margaret and Ann B. Davis as Schultzy. Also known in syndication as *Love That Bob*.

The original casts of The Donna Reed Show and My Three Sons

Our Parents' Favorite Shows

Lawrence Welk, Sing Along With Mitch and Ed Sullivan. In the late 50's when Sullivan began regularly scheduling rock and roll stars, his show became one of our favorites too.

The State Fair in the early fifties. The Mercantile Bank in a photo and in a fifties advertisement.

Two popular bars and one Dallas landmark. The Patio Lounge was a downtown destination and the dance ballroom the It'll Do, was around seemingly since the beginning of time. Honest Joe's Pawnshop was a long-time Deep Ellum fixture.

LIFE

IN
THIS
ISSUE

**LIFE IN DALLAS
IN THE SIXTIES**

The 1960s in Dallas

TV, Rock and Roll, Movies, Restaurants, Sump'n Else, The Studio Club, Skateboards, Surfers A-Go-Go, The Beatles at Memorial Auditorium and so much more...

In Dallas, in the sixties...

In 1962 a Kip's Big Boy Combination Plate (burger, fries and a salad) cost 85¢.

A ticket to see the Beatles in person at Memorial Auditorium was $4 in 1964.

At Lee Optical on Elm Street a pair of glasses including the eye exam ran $12.90.

At the Zuider Zee restaurant on Denton Road the combination seafood platter was 95¢. (1965)

A new 3-bedroom brick home near Hill Junior High School cost $15,000. (1965)

A cherry coke at Skillern's Drug Store soda fountain cost a nickel. (1965)

A six pack of Falstaff Beer cost just 84¢. (1966)

Long playing record albums were $1.49 at Sanger-Harris.

In Garland in 1966 a brand new Dodge Dart cost $1836.

At Bedford's Steak House, a complete steak dinner cost $1.65. (1966)

A gallon of gas at the Texgas Stations was 19¢. (1966)

A Saturday night date wasn't complete without a hot fudge sundae from Kips.

Saturday morning kid shows cost a quarter at The Delman.

Ashburn's Ice Cream raised the price of a cone from 5¢ to 6¢.

Wolfman Jack could be heard nightly in Dallas on radio station XERF broadcasting from Mexico.

The Dallas Texans won the AFL championship in 1962, in a tough game against the Houston Oilers. The Texans defeated the Oilers 20 - 17 in overtime on a 25-yard field goal by Tommy Brooker. Texans' stars included Len Dawson, Fred Arbanas, Abner Haynes, and Jack Spikes.

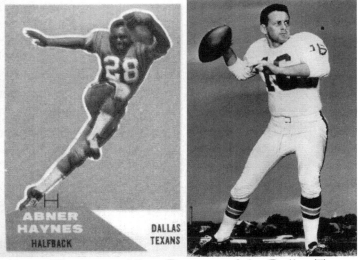

Abner Haynes and Len Dawson of the Dallas Texas

In 1963 The Dallas Texans moved its AFL franchise to Kansas City, becoming The Chiefs.

Teens tried to decide if their fake IDs were good enough to get them into either The Colony Club or The Theater Lounge.

At the Wynnewood Theater, a box of Root Beer Barrels was a nickel, Jr. Mints were a dime and popcorn was 15¢.

On Wednesday nights in 1964, we went to El Fenix for the 65¢ enchilada dinner special.

On January 1, 1966, the Bryan Adams High School Band and Drill Team (The Belles) marched in the Dallas New Years Parade.

The Low Visibility "Low Life"
National dance crazes come and go, but this may be the most localized dance craze in history. From the end of the fifties through the mid-sixties, there was a slow dance called the "low life" which was very popular with local teens. But in fact the dance never spread past two local high schools – Woodrow Wilson and Bryan Adams High School. The dance both pre-dated the twist and outlasted it. At least in two Dallas schools.

Fab

When the Beatles played Dallas in the fall, they stayed at the Cabana Hotel (in the photo below), where the rooms were very high priced -- $14 for a double! That hotel is now a minimum-security jail.

O.L. Nelms Can Just Bite Me

In the early sixties signs began appearing all over town which read "Thanks for helping O.L. Nelms make another million dollars." In answer, one local jokester put up his own sign that read "Thanks for helping Joe Smith make another two bucks." Meanwhile at that time I was earning about 75¢ an hour delivering dry cleaning. I hated O.L. Nelms.

Stores

We shopped at Gibson's Discount Center, Spartan-Atlantic, Fed Mart, Dads and Lads, Ward's Cut Rate Drugs, The Varsity Shop, The Melody Shop, M.E. Moses, Mott's, Wyatt's Grocery, Skillerns's Drugs, Levine's, Margos LaMode, National Shirt Shop, Young Ages, Cabell's DairyWay, Mr. M Stores, E.M. Kahn, Medallion, Rexall Drugs, Titche-Goettingers and White's Department Stores.

CASA LINDA PLAZA SHOPPING VILLAGE

Buckner Blvd. and Garland Road   DA 1-2611

A & A Barber Shop	DA 7-9960	House of Steaks Restaurant	DA 1-8836
Allied Camera Stores	DA 7-6834	Jackson Sporting Goods	DA 7-7344
American Title Company	DA 3-9041	Alene Jones Insurance	DA 1-0349
Ashburn's Ice Cream	DA 7-8934	Marie Krueger, Re-Weaving	DA 7-6848
Robert V. Bailey, D.D.S.	DA 1-6944	Bill Lawrence Real Estate	DA 1-8448
John F. Bell, D.D.S.	DA 7-1954	A. E. Longberry, Tax Consultant	DA 8-2664
Big D Newspaper	DA 7-4514	Maternity Fashions	DA 1-5351
Bill Binford Real Estate	DA 1-2639	W. Kenneth McConnell, Accountant	DA 7-8161
Bob's Play Yard	DA 1-0357	John H. McCullough, M.D.	DA 1-0157
G. M. Boswell, Jr., M.D.	DA 7-6995	Merry-Go-Round Children's Wear	DA 7-7335
Brooks Mays Music Company	DA 8-5654	Miller Shoe Store	DA 1-8655
Burnett, Bruce & Simmons, Attorneys	DA 8-3754	Mr. & Mrs. Gifts	DA 7-1695
C & S Hardware	DA 1-6101	Jack S. Morgan, O.D.	DA 1-5461
Cabell's	DA 7-2233	Mott's 5c & 10c	DA 1-5261
Carpet Land	DA 8-1842	Oregon Mutual Insurance Company	DA 1-1711
Casa Coiffures	DA 8-3262	J. L. Parker Real Estate	DA 1-3670
Casa Linda Barber Shop	DA 7-9716	Patterson Draperies of Dallas	DA 7-5362
Casa Linda Beauty Salon	DA 1-5951	Plaza Coin-A-Wash	DA 7-9909
Casa Linda Billiard Parlor	DA 7-9625	Pollard Gulf Station	DA 7-4242
Casa Linda Coffee Shop	DA 7-9742	Post Office	DA 7-3443
Casa Linda Fashions	DA 1-6582	Radiffe Health Foods	DA 8-9451
Casa Linda Fix-It Shop	DA 4-4168	Reynolds-Penland Men's Wear	DA 1-6411
Casa Linda Kaye	DA 4-4747	Roper & Vance, Architects	DA 1-3656
Casa Linda Paint & Wallpaper	DA 4-4911	Louis Sines, Accountant	DA 1-9750
Casa Linda Realty	DA 1-6401	Skillern Drugs	DA 1-2681
Casa Linda Shoe Repair	DA 7-9960	R. E. Shutt, Real Estate	DA 1-2407
Casa Linda Theatre	DA 1-2141	Jim Smith's Humble Station	DA 4-4464
Char-Mac Beauty Salon	DA 1-6952	Southern Maid Donuts	DA 7-9600
Cinderella Shoppe — Teen Clothing	DA 1-1692	Southern Provident Life Insurance	DA 1-4667
Colbert's Ladies Apparel	DA 4-4441	Spence's #220 Cosmetic Studio	DA 7-1866
Collins Ford Sales	DA 7-6231	State Farm Insurance	DA 1-6244
Commercial Title & Abstract Co.	DA 7-4509	Stewart Title Company	DA 1-2691
Community Sewing Shop	DA 1-5723	Texas Consumers Finance	DA 3-3241
Cornell Cleaners & Laundry	DA 4-4745	Time Jewelers	DA 1-9255
Dulhman Record Shop	DA 4-4546	Yuvin's Bakery	DA 1-0855
Dallas Federal Saving & Loan Assn.	DA 8-6311	Vogue Dress Shop	DA 7-7794
Tom Duncan Insurance	DA 7-5152	Roy Wagoner, M.D.	DA 7-1990
Richard M. Ellis, Jr., D.D.S.	DA 1-3615	Charles C. Wells, Attorney	DA 4-4254
Everett Millinery	DA 7-9735	Horace B. Williams Construction Co.	DA 7-7283
Bob Farrow, Accounting	DA 7-6811	H. Glidden Wilson Insurance	DA 7-9190
Fred's Barbecue	DA 7-3829	Robert H. Wolfe, Attorney	DA 7-4916
Roger H. Godwin, D.D.S.	DA 7-2613	Wyatt Cafeterias	DA 1-0185
H. T. Hayes, M.D.	DA 1-2643	Wyatt Food Stores	DA 1-5330
		Zenith Cleaners	DA 1-5644

In East Dallas out past White Rock Lake, Casa Linda Plaza was a hoppin' place. Check out this list of stores and tenants back in 1964. The first structure in the Plaza was the Casa Linda Theater which was in operation for over fifty years.

White's Stores were all over town in the fifties.
This ad is from November, 1956. Shop early and beat
the Christmas rush. Does any store still
do a "lay-away" plan?

Another chain of stores which were found all over town – M.E. Moses. Along with Ben Franklin, T,G&Y, Mott's and Woolworths, Moses was one of the most popular 5 & 10 stores in the area. This back-to-school ad is from 1959.

More Dallas shopping

Skillern's Drug Stores and Titche's

As Dallas grew, new shopping centers grew all around us. Big Town in Mesquite and Casa View in far East Dallas are two examples.

BIG TOWN SIGN

Largest all-plastic illuminated sign south of Chicago will mark the site of Big Town when the giant shopping, business district opens Feb. 26 at Buckner Boulevard and East Highway 80. From the top of the sign to the ground will be 44 feet and six inches. The sign is 73 feet in length and two feet thick.

Big Town was very proud of this sign - "the largest all-plastic illuminated sign south of Chicago". Apparently there were much larger "part-plastic" signs south of Chicago, as well as some all-plastic non-illuminated signs, and of course a bunch of all-or-part plastic illuminated and non-illuminated signs to the north, east and west of Chicago. But still, I'm sure that this sign was quite a big deal.

Places We Never Went, Honest.

Six Flags Over Texas

Located just west of Dallas in the city of Arlington, Six Flags opened on August 5, 1961. In that first year thousands of park patrons paid $2.75 to discover the wonders of such attractions as The Astro Lift Skyride and LaSalle's Riverboat Ride. (Who could ever forget the untold number of teenaged riverboat guides whose rehearsed speech had them point to two dummy figures hanging in a tree and shout "Look! Up in the tree! It's Jacques and Pierre!").

Original plans called for the park to be known as "Texas Under Six Flags" until someone suggested that Texas has never been "under" anything or anyone.

On less crowded days the huge park is a wonder of fun, attractions and food, although the last time I went, it was so dang crowded that I re-named the place "Six Rides If You're Lucky".

Some of the Six Flags attractions from the sixties included The Log Ride (aka The Flume), The Six Flags Railroad, The Chaparral Cars, The Cave, El Sombrero, Casa Magnetica, The Caddo Canoes, Burro Rides, Stagecoach Ride, Skull Island and the Runaway Mine Train.

ACCENT ON ADVENTURE

SIX FLAGS
OVER TEXAS

**OPEN DAILY
10 a.m.-10 p.m.**

DALLAS / FORT WORTH
TURNPIKE

Six Flags Ad from the '60's

*The Six Flags Railroad circled the entire park making
a stop at the halfway points.*

The "Enco" Happy Motoring cars.

And the less-sporty olde-timey cars.

"Skull Island" was an attraction within the attraction. It was a celebration of the pirate days of the early Texas Gulf Coast.

There they are – count 'em! Six Flags at the entrance.

In the early days, The Six Flags stagecoach used to rumble past "Ghost Town" where skeletons played piano and enjoyed very dry martinis.

The Sky Hook ride hoisted basketsful of park goers high into the air for an aerial view of Six Flags. It towered 200 feet above the Boomtown area of the park.

Charlie and Harrigan

In the early 60s, the popular KLIF morning team, Murphy and Harrigan, changed to Charlie and Harrigan with the departure of Tom Murphy. Jack Woods and Ron Chapman were Charlie and Harrigan respectively. In the mid-60's Woods left and was replaced by a new Charlie, the former KLIF all night DJ, Dan Patrick (McCurdy). Two of the wild characters created on this show were "Herman Whirlitzer" and the not-very-politically-correct "Manuel Labor". Ron Chapman went on to TV programs and a long stint at KVIL. Chapman continued on Dallas radio into the 21st Century. Dan McCurdy moved to rival KBOX where he hosted a top rated morning show, before going on to a successful advertising career in the Dallas area.

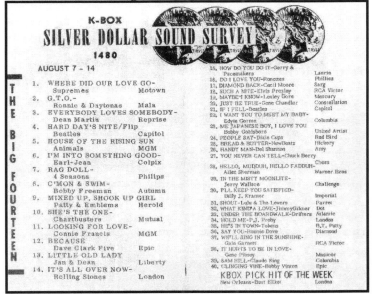

A KBOX Top 40 Survey from August 1964

KLIF TOP 40
HITS OF THE WEEK!

50,000 WATTS @ 1190 / SUBSCRIBED BY MORE THAN 200 RECORD DISTRIBUTORS

JANUARY 18, 1964

#	Song	Artist	Label
1	NITTY GRITTY	SHIRLEY ELLIS	CONGRESS
2	MIDNIGHT MARY	JOEY POWERS	AMY
3	THERE I'VE SAID IT AGAIN	BOBBY VINTON	EPIC
4	HEY LITTLE COBRA	RIP CHORDS	COLUMBIA
5	OUT OF LIMITS	MARKETTS	W B
6	YOU DON'T OWN ME	LESLIE GORE	MERCURY
7	WHISPERING	A. STEVENS-N. TEMPO	ATCO
8	ALL IN THE GAME	CLIFF RICHARD	EPIC
9	LOUIE, LOUIE	KINGSMEN	WAND
10	UM UM UM UM UM UM	MAJOR LANCE	OKAY
11	LETTER FROM SHERRY	DALE WARD	DOT
12	I WANNA HOLD YOUR HAND	BEATLES	CAPITOL
13	FOR YOU	RICK NELSON	DECCA
14	TRA LA LA LA SUZY	DEAN & JEAN	RUST
15	GIRLS GROW UP FASTER THAN BOYS	COOKIES	DEMENSION
16	SOMEWHERE	TYMES	PARKWAY
17	TALKIN' ABOUT YOU	STEVE & EDIE	COLUMBIA
18	DAISY PETAL PICKIN'	JIMMY GILMER	DOT
19	HE SAYS THE SAME THINGS TO ME	SKEETER DAVIS	R C A
20	CALIFORNIA SUN	RIVIERAS	RIVIERA
21	LUCKY OLE SUN	RAY CHARLES	A B C
22	SOUTHTOWN U. S. A.	DIXIEBELLES	SOUND STAGE
23	A FOOL NEVER LEARNS	ANDY WILLIAMS	COLUMBIA
24	POPSICLES & ICICLES	MURMAIDS	CHATTAHOOCI
25	PUPPY LOVE	BARBARA LEWIS	ATLANTIC
26	HARLEM SHUFFLE	BOB & EARL	MARC
27	YOUNG & IN LOVE	CHRIS CROSBY	M G M
28	I HAVE A BOYFRIEND	CHIFFONS	LAURIE
29	FUNNY LITTLE CLOWN	BOBBY GOLDSBORO	U A
30	MAYBELLINE	MATT LUCAS	DOT
31	MY WORST HABIT	JOHNNY ELGIN	KASH
32	WHAT KIND OF FOOL DO YOU THINK I AM	TAMS	A B C
33	ABIGALE BEECHER	FREDDIE CANNON	W B
34	MILLER'S CAVE	BOBBY BARE	R C A
35	WOW WOWEE	ANGELS	SMASH
36	ONLY WANT TO BE WITH YOU	DUSTY SPRINGFIELD	PHILLIPS
37	BEGGIN TO YOU	MARTY ROBBINS	COLUMBIA
38	CUSTOM MACHINE	BRUCE & TERRY	COLUMBIA
39	WELCOME TO MY WORLD	JIM REEVES	R C A
40	VAYA CON DIOS	DRIFTERS	ATLANTIC

KLIF KING KLIMBER...

****LONG GONE LONESOME BLUES**** HANK WILLIAMS, JR. M G M

January 18, 1964

The KBOX Disc-Jockey lineup for 1966. Dan Patrick had been on KLIF as the all-night guy, was promoted to being Charlie of 'Charlie and Harrigan' and then was lured away to be the morning man on KBOX.

The Curiously Confused Caller

In 1967 KLIF radio ran a late night call-in talk show called "The Snake Pit" with its host Chuck Boyle. One night in the late summer I was listening as something really wonderful happened. The hot topics of the show that night included the death of American Nazi leader George Lincoln Rockwell, the recent release of The Beatles' "Sergeant Pepper" album and the escalation of bombing in Southeast Asia. With all of these topics swirling together in his head, one confused caller rang the show and asked the host "Hey Chuck, just who is this Sgt. Culpepper who's been droppin' bombs on Rockwall?"

Record Stores

Above: The Melody Shop in NorthPark. Fondly recalled stores around town: The Dallasan in Casa Linda, Preston Records, The Record Mart downtown and The Top Ten in Oak Cliff.

The Boy Who Didn't Exist

In the fall of 1963, while bored in Home Room at Bryan Adams High School, four friends and I invented a student named Frederick Richard Lambert. We signed him up for the student directory and a boatload of student activities and clubs. He joined not only The Future Red Raiders and The Future SMU Mustangs but also The Future Texas Longhorns and The Future A&M Aggies. He was also an official member of almost every school organization with the exception of the drill team

The next year we invented his twin sister Frieda Lambert and entered her name in the contest for School Sweetheart. My buddy Steve and I spent a long weekend making the posters that would grace the halls of B.A. urging students to vote for Frieda. Instead of the pretty images and charming photos that filled the other candidates' posters, we looked for the ugliest, worst photos we could find. From Life Magazine we cut out pictures of insects, train wrecks and disasters, pasted them onto the poster boards with the words: "Vote for Frieda Lambert." We were told that Frieda drew enough votes to be first runner up, but she had to withdraw when the administration discovered that she didn't actually exist.

In the spring of '65 we signed Freddie up for his official senior picture to appear in the annual. In his biography, we dutifully listed each and every club he had joined, and added a few sports teams to make him appear macho. In the summer, when the paperwork came to my house for Freddie to come to Gary's Studio in Casa View for his portrait, I realized that I had no one daring enough to pose for the picture. Enter Bryan, one of our close friends. He combed his hair the opposite direction, put on my glasses and he and I went to Gary's Studio for his picture. I still have the photo receipt in my collection of worthless ephemera. Bryan's photo as Freddie duly appeared in the annual, the glorious cap to Freddie's four year high school career.

But we failed in our attempt to get him graduated. A co-conspirator on the Diploma Committee actually had a real, authentic diploma made up in the name of Frederick Richard Lambert. Unfortunately, during the ceremony, the assistant principal realized that no such student appeared on his official list of graduates and stuck the diploma under the table. I never thought to sneak up to the stage after the ceremony and get it, but I would pay $1000 for that diploma today.

LAMBERT, FREDERICK RICHARD
"Fred"
May 6, 1948; Delphi, India
Majors: English, History, Math, Science
Student Council, German Club, Science Club, Art Club, Latin Club, J.C.T.C., Rally Club, Pub Staff, Honor Class, O,R,I, Football, Baseball, Track, Folk Music Club, Youth for Christ, Baseball, Basketball, Red Cross, Future Red Raiders, Cothurnus Club, P.T.A. rep., Swim Team, Tactics Club, Lab Assistant, Math Club, Ice Skating Club, Honor Roll, Orchestra, Historical Society, A.F.S., Para-Medical Club, Key Club, Senior Play

Random Memory Flashes from the 60s

Charco's
Goss on Ross ("The Tradin' Hoss")
Studio club drink chips
The Lady of the Lake
Kat's Karavan
Orange Julius
Miss Inez playing the organ at Luby's Cafeteria
Sunset Bay at White Rock Lake
Y.Y. Wickie on 7-Eleven commercials
Drinking a "Big Shake" at Skillerns
Fair Day
The Weird Beard
Art Grindel's Used Cars ("I Want To Sell YOU A Car!")
Shindig and Hullaballoo
Wolf Man Jack
Nightmare Theater
Live concerts at Lee Park
Watching planes land at the observation deck of Love
    Field
Ports o' Call
The Wilshire Theater
The Lloyd Thaxton Show
Frank Jolle on KBOX
Green Valley Raceway
The Penguin Drive In in Oak Cliff
Putt-Putt Golf
Camp Wisdom
Stoney Burns
The Fair Park Ice Arena
Pommac
Krystal Hamburgers

Hollywood on the Trinity

ONLY *HELL* COULD BREED SUCH AN ENORMOUS BEAST... ONLY *GOD* COULD DESTROY IT!

THE GIANT GILA MONSTER

DON **SULLIVAN** • LISA **SIMONE**
Fred Graham • Shug Fisher
Produced by KEN CURTIS • Directed by RAY KELLOGG
A McLendon Radio Pictures Release

In 1967 Warren Beatty produced and starred in the now-classic movie "Bonnie and Clyde" filmed largely in Dallas and the surrounding area. The movie, directed by Arthur Penn, was not well liked by The Warner Brothers company executives and was sent directly to the drive-in and small theater circuits. However, positive word-of-mouth advertising helped the movie to become one of the highest grossing pictures in the history of Warner Brothers. The film was eventually nominated for 10 Academy Awards and won four New York Film Critics Awards. Many historical Dallas area locations (most of which are gone now, unfortunately) can be seen in the film.

Through the sixties, Dallas was a center for low-budget motion picture making. A few big-budget hits like "State Fair" (1961) and "Bonnie and Clyde" (1967) also filmed in Dallas. Beginning in the mid-seventies, many larger budget films began to be produced in the area. But any list of truly classy movies filmed substantially in the Dallas area prior to 1980 would have to include:

Go Down Death (1944)
Of One Blood (1944)
Dirty Gertie of Harlem USA (1946)
Free White and 21 (1963)
Jivin' In Bebop (1946)
The Girl In Room 20 (1946)
Juke Joint (1947)
Rock Baby Rock It (1957)
The Giant Gila Monster (1959)
The Killer Shrews (1959)
My Dog Buddy (1959)
Beyond The Time Barrier (1960)
State Fair (1961)
Free White and 21 (1963)
The Trial of Lee Harvey Oswald (1964)
Under Age (1964)
High Yellow (1965)
The Black Cat (1966)
Curse of the Swamp Creature (1966)
Zontar The Thing From Venus (1966)
Mars Needs Women (1967)
Creature Of Destruction (1967)
Night Fright (1967)
In The Year 2889 (1967)
Bonnie and Clyde (1967)
Hell Raiders (1968)
It's Alive (1969)
Bullet For Pretty Boy (1970)
Mark of the Witch (1970)
Don't Look In The Basement (1973)
Phantom of the Paradise (1974)
Horror High (1974)
Poor White Trash II (1974)

Drive In (1976)
Return To Boggy Creek (1977)
The Seniors (1978)
Don't Open The Door (1980)

Below: Posters for two Dallas-made movies

Above: One of the most exciting scenes from Dallas-made "Mars Needs Women" – a Martian stands around talking about how he really needs women. All the guys I knew in Dallas at the time needed women too, and as far as we were concerned, Mars could just get in line.

Left: *Rock Baby Rock It* – the greatest rock and roll movie ever made. (OK that's just not true. But it may have been the best rock and roll movie made in Dallas in 1957, since it was the only one.) It starred local rockabilly king Johnny Carroll.

And another all-time Big D biggie – *The Killer Shrews*. It proved the idea that if you take big dogs and paste cardboard fangs on their faces and cover them with carpet scraps you've got the makings of a movie that people will still talk about over fifty years later.

Lewisville Pop Festival

Less than a month after the famous Woodstock Music Festival in New York, promoter Angus Wynne III roped in some big-time performers to take the temporary stage of the Lewisville International Pop Festival. The event took place from August 30 through September 1, 1969 at the Dallas International Motor Speedway a few miles outside of Dallas.

Internationally-known artists such as Janis Joplin, Led Zeppelin, Chicago, B.B. King, Sly and the Family Stone, Johnny Winter, Grand Funk Railroad and many more top name acts attracted about 120,000 music fans to the three-day festival, all for around six bucks a ticket.

Though some local residents were shocked by a bit of occasional nude swimming in the nearby lake and by some reported drug use, no violence or major negative incidents were reported.

Janis Joplin

The Lady of The Lake

One of Dallas most enduring and intriguing urban legends involves a ghostly apparition known as The Lady of the Lake. Although some sources date the legend as early as 1915 or so, most stories of the ill-fated young woman set the event in the twenties.

The story usually begins with a motorist (sometimes referred to as a cab driver) who picks up a young woman in distress one late night at White Rock Lake. The woman is dressed in a white party dress that is soaked with water. As she gets into the back seat of the car she tells the driver that she has been in a boating accident on the lake and asks to be taken to her home. The driver gets the address and drives the woman to the house. However, when he looks into the back seat the mysterious young woman is gone, and only a puddle of water remains where she had been sitting.

The driver knocks on the door of the house and explains the situation to the older man who answers. The older man informs the driver that his story is a cruel joke.

"My daughter died in a boating accident on White Rock Lake one year ago tonight," the older man informs the driver.

Did it really happen? Who knows. Generations of Dallasites have told the story in complete seriousness. And if it did happen, it happened at White Rock Lake in Dallas

On the next page: two articles from The Dallas Morning News in the 1960's. The Lady of the Lake was still active in those days!

Riot Squads Called Out in 'Ghost Hunt'

By JAMES EWELL

A midnight ghost hunt promoted by radio talk-show personality Chuck Boyles sent an estimated 200 to 250 carloads of youths streaming into White Rock Lake Park early Thursday, so alarming police that riot-trained officers were called out.

Police barricaded Cox Cemetery in the park to prevent an estimated 1,000 youths from overruning the pioneer burial site in search of White Rock Lake's mythical "lady of the lake" ghost.

Two dozen men of the riot-trained special enforcement detail were rushed to the park on West Lawther Drive in Northeast Dallas when the youths began heckling and tossing coins at officers behind the barricades. Not until 15 additional helmeted police arrived in a 4-car motorcade did the crowd begin to disintegrate about 2:30 a.m.

Two persons were arrested for throwing lighted firecrackers.

Police Capt. William R. Fulghum said the crowd was noisy but never got out of hand.

Fulghum, in his report to superiors, said the crowd was made up of youths between 13 and 20 years old.

In all, police massed 47 officers at two points in the park to restrain the flow of cars. The resulting traffic jamup brought the youths out of their cars to form lines opposite the police barricades. The crowd was joined by a 50-car motorcade which had formed at the radio station's downtown studio.

Boyles, whose late-night show on station KLIF frequently deals with controversial issues, showed up at the park incognito after promising listeners a public appearance.

"To have presented myself before the adoring crowd would certainly have caused a full scale riot," Boyles explained in a later broadcast in which he also apologized to police.

'Ghost' Hunt Poses Police Headache

Several hundred teen-agers, massing for a gigantic search for the mythical "lady of the lake ghost," converged on White Rock Lake late Wednesday night and early Thursday morning, posing a king-size traffic problem for police.

Squads of police were at the scene trying to block access roads from the carloads of youths apparently replying to a radio station broadcast that one of its announcers would lead them in a search for the oft-rumored ghost.

But as soon as one road was blocked, the cars headed for another.

At 1:30 a.m. Thursday, special police enforcement squads and overtime units were massed at the police garage to go by caravan to the scene in an attempt to barricade Lawther Drive, which encircles the lake. More than 100 carloads of youths were reported trying to enter the lakefront drive at that time.

Dallas At The Movies

Fondly remembered indoor movie theaters in Dallas included

Residential:

Arcadia
Big Town Cinema
Casa Linda
Circle
Coronet
Crest
Delman
Electra
Ervay
Esquire
Festival
Fine Arts
Forest
Granada
Grand
Heights
Inwood
Knox
Lagow
Lakewood
Lido
Lochwood
Medallion
NorthPark Cinema
Park Forest
Pleasant Grove
Preston Royal
Ridgewood (in Garland)

State
Stevens
Sunset
Texas
Varsity
Village
Vogue
Wilshire
Wynnewood

Downtown:
Capri
Majestic
Melba
Palace
Tower

Left: The wonderful 1930's-era art deco wall paintings inside the Lakewood Theater.
Right: The Village Theater in the sixties.

Drive-In Movies

The fifties decade was also the golden age of the drive-in movie theater, which began as an ideal place to take the family, complete with a playground and snack bar. But soon American teenagers, now mobile in their own automobiles, discovered that the drive-in was much more than a place to see movies. It also provided them with a license to neck, without fear of the police or park patrol hassling them at the local lake. Teens realized that they could smuggle in a six pack of beer (and a few of their friends in the trunk), and be entertained by a double feature and each other, for about a buck.

As drive-ins sprung up all over the country, the competition for the teen audiences became fierce. This led to triple-and-quadruple features ("dusk to dawn" on the weekends) and a scramble for films that appealed to teen audiences. Theater owners soon noticed that if they were running an Audie Murphy double feature and the drive-in down the street was featuring two teen-oriented films, that the biggest boxoffice business went to the teenage flicks.

Supplying a demand has always been the basic formula for any business, and the smaller American independent film companies were ready, willing and chomping at the bit to supply drive-ins and smaller "hard-top" theaters with all the teen product they could use.

What did the teens want? Horror films, rock musicals and movies starring teenagers doing heretofore forbidden things on the screen. Drag racing, motorcycle madness, teenage dances, fast cars, loose girls and a cinematic freedom-to-do-whatever that had never been shown to teens on movie screens before. As wild as these things sound, it was still the fifties, and these movies were as naïve and non-threatening as the times required. But still, the subject matter seemed so uninhibited to the terribly inhibited teens at the time. Thus a mild little movie like *Hot-Rod Girl* could fill the drive-in to capacity.

One of the earliest drive-in movie horror films aimed at teens was *The Beast With a Million Eyes*. It was seen and enjoyed by about a million teens, even thought the beast of the misleading title actually had only two eyes.

The combination of teens and terror continued throughout drive-in flick history. In the mid-fifties titles like *Motorcycle Gang, Dragstrip Riot, Reform School Girl, The Sinister*

Urge, Runaway Daughters and *High School Confidential* alternated with such releases as *The She Creature, The Screaming Skull, The Undead, Invasion of the Saucer Men* and *Teenagers From Outer Space.* Early rock movies like *The Girl Can't Help It, Rock Rock Rock* and *Rock All Night* gave teens the chance to hear and see their music.

In the early sixties, drive-ins drew boxoffice blood with a string of elegant and successful Roger Corman films inspired by the works of Edgar Allen Poe (*The Pit and The Pendulum, The Premature Burial* and others.) By the mid-sixties we had The Beach Party era and a new style of rock documentary begun by a filmed concert entitled *The TAMI Show.* In 1967 a new boom of teens had arrived and the mood was changing. Biker films, hippie movies and a new more violent (and raunchier) style of movie was in vogue. Titles like *The Wild Angels* and *Wild In The Streets* filled the theaters.

By the seventies, the drive-in theater concept began losing steam and the number of outdoor screens shrunk each year. Today it is difficult to find a drive-in theater although a few gallantly struggle on in the era of the home video and the multiplex mall cinema.

Rock and Roll Flicks

Most rock and roll movies of the fifties (and early sixties) are dreadful, let's be honest and state that right up front. As movies they suck.

The formula for most of these flicks was simple: Boy meets guitar, boy loses car race, boy wins talent show. Mix in several musical numbers by whichever act is hot that month. Edit using garden shears with your eyes closed. Release to drive-in theaters and make a bundle. To be fair to the teen audiences who went to the drive-in to see these films – we knew that these were crummy movies and simply didn't care. For one thing, even if the drive-in had been showing industrial training films, the teens probably would have gone anyway. The drive-in theater was a whole lot more than a place to see movies. And for another thing, in the fifties teens had little opportunity to see rock and roll stars perform. An occasional act on TV, a very rare concert in town and drive-in rock and roll flicks provided all the visual exposure that rockers had at the time. So, any movie with the word "rock" in the title and a familiar musical name in the credits would pack the theaters. The movies were not required to be good or even passable.

Especially in the early days. That's why some of the worst/best films ever made are fifties rock movies. Among the very worst/best are *Rock All Night, Don't Knock The Rock* and *Hot Rod Gang*. The collective budget for these flicks was probably about $8.27, the acting was stiff, the writing was awful, the direction was mostly "point the camera that way." But these movies had two elements that appealed greatly to teens

The two things that made these terrible films so wonderful to teen audiences are easy to understand in hindsight. First, there was just the simple fact that the movies showed teenagers who were doing whatever they wanted and having fun in the process. This was very unusual in movies prior to the fifties. Sure, back in the forties Andy Hardy liked to drive around in his jalopy and whistle at the girls, but deep down in his heart his attitude was always revealed in a sloppily sentimental heart-to-heart chat with his dad, Judge Hardy. "Gee whiz, Dad," Andy would blubber. "You're so wise and wonderful and I'm just a dumb kid." Since mankind crawled out of caves, teenagers of each generation would not believe drivel of this sort even for a moment. Teenagers then, now and always have an attitude that says "Aw what do you know? You're old, I'm young. I know everything!"

Finally, in the fifties, filmmakers discovered this pool of untapped teen angst and began to pump it for all it was worth. Which was a bundle. Even though in the end, the movie teens usually had some small comeuppance and were forced to admit that at least a few of the parents weren't total idiots, for the 70 or so minutes prior to this, the teens had the run of the world. And, in the end, their movie parents were forced to admit that the teens had been right all along – that rock and roll wasn't bad or that car racing was downright swell or whatever conclusion that the premise of the movie had led them to.

Movies had never before created a world where the kids were right and the parents had to admit it. This was an incredibly appealing fantasy to the restless teens of the mid-fifties.

The second reason these bad films are so good is the music. As stated above, some of the greatest talents in rock and roll lent their talents to these fifties-era flicks. Musical segments by The Platters, Bill Haley and the Comets, Little Richard, Chuck Berry, Fats Domino, The Treniers, Eddie Cochran, Gene Vincent and the Blue Caps and dozens of other hot rockers enlivened the screen in a way that their few small screen TV appearances could not. Teens could neck during the insipid plot portion of the movie, and sit up and take notice during the rock portions, the car chases and the inevitable scene that vindicated the teenage heroes.

All for one dollar a carload.

Horrors and hot rods, beach blasts and wild girls –
four of the subjects that filled the Dallas drive-ins of
the fifties and sixties.

A LIST OF EVERY DRIVE IN
THEATER IN DALLAS
1940's - 1980's

183 DRIVE-IN THEATRE – In Irving.

APOLLO DRIVE-IN - The Apollo drive-in was in Garland off LBJ Freeway and was previously known as The Garland Road Drive In.

ARAPAHO DRIVE-IN THEATRE – In Richardson

ASTRO DRIVE-IN – Opened in 1965 on South Walton Walker Blvd. at Kiest.

BELT LINE 67 – Highway 67, where else?

BIG "D" DRIVE-IN – Was located on Harry Hines Blvd.

BRUTON ROAD DRIVE-IN THEATRE- at the five points intersection of Bruton Rd, Peachtree and Sam Houston Road. Eventually destroyed by a tornado in the 1980s.

BUCKNER BLVD. DRIVE-IN - 3333 North Buckner Boulevard at John West Road. The giant clown face front was painted by artist Reed Hubnell.

CASA VIEW DRIVE-IN – Built in the fifties at the corner of Gus Thomasson and Maylee Blvd, near Casa View Shopping Center

CENTURY DRIVE IN – In Grand Prairie near Oak Cliff on the spot where the Downs Drive-In had been.

CHALK HILL DRIVE-IN – An early Dallas drive-in, it opened back in 1941 on West Davis Street.

CINDERELLA / KING DRIVE-IN - On South Lamar. It began as the Cinderella Drive-in and was changed to the King drive-in.

COUNTRY SQUIRE – Near Redbird Airport

DENTON ROAD DRIVE-IN -11325 Harry Hines Blvd.

DOWNS DRIVE -IN– Grand Prairie

GARLAND ROAD DRIVE IN – Became the Apollo on Garland Road

GEMINI TWIN - North Central Expressway at Forest Lane, this huge twin screen April 15, 1965.

HAMPTON ROAD DRIVE-IN - Guess where this one was. Right! On Hampton Road!

HI VUE- In Oak Cliff on Beckley Avenue.

JEFFERSON DRIVE-IN THEATRE- On West Jefferson, this was an early drive-in, built in 1949.

KING DRIVE-IN - See Cinderella

KAUFMAN PIKE -C.F. Hawn freeway in Pleasant Grove. Another drive-in which featured a circus-themed screen.

KIEST BLVD – Another giveaway – yep, located on Kiest Boulevard.

LINDA KAY DRIVE-IN – Hawn Freeway

LONE STAR DRIVE-IN - Lawnview Avenue it began as a regular family drive-in and ended as a porn theater.

NORTHWEST HIGHWAY- NW Highway at Hillcrest. This was Dallas' first drive-in theater, opened in 1941.

PARK PLAZA DRIVE–IN – It was located in Irving.

PLANO DRIVE IN – Central at Parker. Seemed like it was way out in the boonies back then.

REBEL TWIN DRIVE-IN – In Carrollton.

SAMUELL BLVD. DRIVE-IN - OK, I'm gonna quit telling you where these theaters were. Yes, this one was on Samuel Boulevard, Sherlock!

SOUTH LOOP DRIVE-IN – It opened in 1950 and featured Snow White and the Seven Dwarves painted on the exterior of the screen.

STARLITE – On South Lamar

TEXAS STADIUM DRIVE-IN – Multi-screen theater which utilized the Texas Stadium parking lot whenever another event was not scheduled.

TOWN & COUNTRY DRIVE-IN – On Plano Road in the Lake Highlands section.

THE TWIN (East and West) – Dallas' first double screen outdoor theater located at Jefferson Boulevard and Davis.

We Owe The Buckner Drive-In Eight Bucks

One night in spring of 1964 at the Dairy Queen in our neighborhood, a group of high school boys were standing around doin' nothin' (what we did best) when we discovered that we had one dollar between all of us. What could nine guys do for one buck? Buy twenty small Cokes at a nickel a pop? We could get one six pack of Falstaff (99¢) at Doug's Bait Store by the spillway...but less than one full beer each sounded like a waste of a buck. And anyway none of us had a fake ID or the guts to use it if we had one.

Then we came up with the idea! The admission price for one person at the Buckner Drive-In was one dollar! We could try and sneak EIGHT guys into the theater in one car! It would be a world record (as far as we knew or cared.)

The biggest car in the group belonged to my buddy Mark. It was a late '50s model Mercury soft-top convertible and was about two blocks long. Bus drivers looked longingly at Mark's car wishing that their vehicle was as long as his.

The real trick was getting eight big, clunky high school sophomore boys hidden in one car. The car was big, but not big enough to comfortably hide eight guys. The key word is "comfortably". We got all eight of us into the vehicle - after several loadings, unloadings and foldings of our bodies.

Mark took the back seat out and we put a few of us in under and behind it. Then we sealed those poor guys under and behind that back seat while we packed the rest of us into various nooks of the car. It must have felt like being entombed.

Two guys were laying on the floor in the back seat covered by a blanket. Three more were in the trunk. The last of us was our friend Ronny and he simply could not find a space left on that car to hide in. About all that was available at that stage was the glove box. So Ronny crawled into the folds of the soft top convertible (the top was down) which was all piled up on the front part of the top of the trunk. He could not quite fit in and part of his left arm and hand stuck out. So we wrapped a white T-shirt around that arm and hoped it would blend in with the white color of the car.

With all of us crammed into dark, smelly crevices in the car, Mark drove off toward the theater. Although he swore he did not, we were convinced that he took the longest possible route to get there. It seemed like we were folded into that car for hours. Then we heard Mark yell to us "OK, we're pulling up to the ticket booth...everybody shut up and lay still!"

I was one of the idiots crammed into the trunk and I began to wonder how the attendant could possibly miss seeing Ronny's arm sticking out of the convertible top. I began rehearsing my excuse speech so I could have it ready when my Dad came down to bail me out of jail. I also wondered what would happen if they impounded the car and forgot to look in the trunk. How long would it take for them to discover our bodies?

Then the car started moving again and in about a minute the trunk popped open and Mark was letting us out. Eight 16 year old boys emerged from that car in about two seconds. To anyone who was watching from the very back row of the drive-in we must have looked like that tiny clown car in the circus from which a dozen clowns get out.

If I remember correctly the movie was a real stinker and we didn't even watch it. The real goal had been accomplished - the sneaking in of eight guys in one car. After an hour or so of building the accomplishment up in our minds until it had achieved the legendary status it obviously deserved, we left and drove back to the DQ to brag and strut.

When we got the Dairy Queen everyone had left. So we stood around for a minute and then just went home. We didn't get to brag and strut - which would have been the best part - but at least we didn't get arrested.

And to this day we hold the World's Record for "the most high school sophomores to sneak into The Buckner Boulevard Drive-In Theater in one Mercury convertible". A mighty impressive feat...

The Early Days of the Drive-In in Dallas

The very first drive-n theater in Dallas was The Northwest Highway, opened in 1941 at Hillcrest and Northwest Highway.

Drive-ins started as a family concept, a place to bring the kids, complete with playgrounds. By our high school years, drive-ins had become "passion pits" and many a parent refused to let their teenage kids attend one. (We went anyway.)

In the fifties the classic local drive-ins did not show teen-oriented movies, but double or triple features, usually regular family fare. The first film of the evening was usually the lightest-weight family film, and the dramas and action films came later as the kids began to curl up to sleep in the back seat.

This photo courtesy of J-Bar at Wikipedia Commons

New Drive-In Theater Makes Its Bow Friday

The Buckner Boulevard, Dallas' newest drive-in motion picture theater will open at 6:45 p.m. Friday with "Tycoon," Technicolor film starring John Wayne and Laraine Day as the opening attraction. The new outdoor theater, located at Buckner Boulevard between Samuel Boulevard and East Grand Avenue, has all the latest features including individual speakers for every automobile, a children's playground, outdoor seats for those who wish to get out of the cars, and a large snack bar. Frank Tharp is manager of the new house, which is owned and operated by Underwood and Ezell.

New Garland Road Drive-In Theater To Open Friday

Typical Hollywood fanfare, complete with giant searchlights and a circus calliope tableau band wagon, will attend the opening Friday night of the Garland Road Drive-In Theater. Charla will play the decorative calliope prior to the showing of "Oh, Your Beautiful Doll," with June Haver and Mark Stevens, at 7:30 p.m.

The theater, located at Garland and Shiloh Roads, is the first of three new drive-ins to be opened by Leon Theatres this month. The Hampton Road Drive-In, across from Kiest Park, and the Denton Road Drive-In, at Denton Drive and Joe Field Road, will begin operations in the near future, according to C. D. Leon, owner.

New Drive-Ins were built throughout the fifties — The Lone Star, The Samuel Blvd, The Garland Road (which became the Apollo in the late 60's)

When the Buckner Drive In was built, very little else existed way out there in the sticks. The area of Casa Linda had not been built and of course neighboring Casa View and Lochwood were not even in the planning stages. There was a small airport down John West Road from the theater and patrons used to watch planes swoop down over their cars heading toward the landing strip.

DRIVE-IN THEATRES

★ THERE'S ONE IN YOUR NEIGHBORHOOD ★

ARAPAHO
600 Arapaho Road
Richardson
AD 5-6515

First Dallas Run
"COUNTRY MUSIC
ON BROADWAY"
Color—Hank Williams
"PT-109"
Color—Cliff Robertson

"GREAT SPY MISSION"
7:15-10:45—Sophia Loren
Color—George Peppard
"MAIL ORDER BRIDE"
9:20—Buddy Ebsen

HAMPTON RD.
Across from Kiest Park
FE 1-0411

BELT LINE — 67
Intersection
Belt Line Rd. and
Hwy. 67, N.E.
BR 9-8381

"PARDNERS"
7:05-10:34—Dean Martin
Jerry Lewis
"LIVING IT UP"
8:55—Dean Martin
Jerry Lewis

Show Starts at 7:10
"SONS OF KATIE ELDER"
Color—John Wayne
Dean Martin
"BOY 10 FEET TALL"
Color—Edw. G. Robinson

HI-VUE
5601 South
Thornton Expressway
FR 1-1991

BIG "D"
No. of Inwood Rd.
on Hines
ME 7-1142

First Dallas Showing
"COUNTRY MUSIC
ON BROADWAY"
7:15-11:30—Color
"CIMMARON"
9:05—Glenn Ford
Color—Maria Schell

"PARDNERS"
7:15-10:42—Dean Martin
Color—Jerry Lewis
"LIVING IT UP"
9:08—Dean Martin
Color—Jerry Lewis

JEFFERSON
4506 W. Jefferson
FE 1-1981

BRUTON RD.
at Five Points
AT 5-4017

"COUNTRY MUSIC
ON BROADWAY"
7:15-10:45—Color
Hank Williams Jr.
"THE LIVELY SET"
9:10—James Darren
Pamela Tiffin

Two Dean Martin and
Jerry Lewis Hits
"PARDNERS"
Color 7:15-10:35
"LIVING IT UP"
9:00—Color

KAUFMAN PIKE
Hwy 175 at Jim Miller Rd
EX 1-8145

BUCKNER BLVD.
Buckner Blvd. West of
Garland Hwy. 67 and of
DA 3-6376

All Color Program
"PARDNERS"
7:00—Martin & Lewis
"LIVING IT UP"
8:55—Martin & Lewis
"FUN IN ACAPULCO"
10:40—Elvis Presley

$1.50 Admits Carload
"HIGH YELLOW"
7:15—All Star Cast
"BLACK SPURS"
Rory Calhoun

KIEST BLVD.
3100 East Kiest at
Southerland
WH 2-4133

CASA VIEW
Gus Thomasson Road
BR 9-7076

First Dallas Run
"COUNTRY MUSIC
ON BROADWAY"
Color—Hank Williams Jr.
"SEX & SINGLE GIRL"
Color—Natalie Wood

$1.50 Admits Carload
"RAIDERS FROM BENEATH
THE SEA"—7:15
"DUEL AT APACHE WELLS"
"INCREDIBLE SHRINKING
MAN"

LINDA KAY
Highway 175
AT 6-4751

CHALK HILL
4501 West Davis
on Fort Worth Pike
FE 1-6041

All Color Program
"PARDNERS"
7:00—Martin & Lewis
"LIVING IT UP"
8:45—Martin & Lewis
"FUN IN ACAPULCO"
10:15—Elvis Presley

"COUNTRY MUSIC
ON BROADWAY"
7:15-10:51—Buck Owens
Color—Hank Williams Jr.
"THE LIVELY SET"
9:16—Pamela Tiffin
Color—James Darren

LONE STAR
Lawnview at
Forney Rd.
EV 1-0357

The
COUNTRY SQUIRE
3 Mi. So. Redbird Airport
Hwy. 67 South

"GREAT SPY MISSION"
7:50-11:00—Sophia Loren
Color—Geo. Peppard
"BUS RILEY'S BACK
IN TOWN"—9:15
Color—Ann Margret

"VON RYAN'S EXPRESS"
7:00-11:00—Frank Sinatra
Color—Trevor Howard
"DEAR BRIGITTE"
9:20 Only
Color—James Stewart

183 DRIVE-IN
Britain Rd. and Hwy. 183
In Irving—BL4 9702

DENTON RD.
Hines Blvd. North of Carle
CH 7-2175

All Color Program
"PARDNERS"
7:00—Martin & Lewis
"LIVING IT UP"
8:47—Martin & Lewis
"FUN IN ACAPULCO"
10:22—Elvis Presley

Great Spy Mission
"OPERATION CROSSBOW"
7:00-11:20—Sophia Loren
Color—George Peppard
"A TICKLISH AFFAIR"
9:45 Only
Red Buttons, Shirley Jones

PARK PLAZA
4100 Carpenter Freeway West
(Formerly Hwy. 183)
Irving — BL3-3596

DOWNS
2816 W. Main—Hwy. 80
Grand Prairie
AN 2-1431

"COUNTRY MUSIC
ON BROADWAY"
7:15-10:55—Hank Snow
Color—Hank Williams Jr.
"MESQUERADE"
9:15 Only—Cliff Robertson
Color—Jack Hawkins

Opens at 6:30 P.M.
"OPERATION CROSSBOW"
7:00-10:50—Sophia Loren
Color—George Peppard
"KISSIN' COUSINS"
9:14—Elvis Presley
Pamela Tiffin

SOUTH LOOP
Ledbetter between
Lancaster and Lamar
FR 1-1500

GARLAND RD.
Garland Rd. at Shiloh Rd.
BR 8-5600

"OPERATION CROSSBOW"
7:05-10:51—Sophia Loren
Color—George Peppard
"THE ROUNDERS"
9:26—Glenn Ford
Color—Henry Fonda

"PARDNERS"
7:10-10:30—Dean Martin
Color—Jerry Lewis
"LIVING IT UP"
8:50—Dean Martin
Color—Jerry Lewis

**TOWN
&
COUNTRY**
AD 3-5040
Plano Rd. - Forrest Ln.

A Dallas Drive-In lineup from 1965

The Sixties

Although the first drive-in theaters arrived in Dallas in the forties and began to proliferate in the fifties, the sixties were the heyday of the local drive-in.

The drive-in was the place to go even if you didn't have a hot date. Carloads of teens would descend on the local "ozoner" each weekend night, strolling around, honking our horns, switching cars and generally ruining the night for those who actually came to see movies. We usually brought our own food and snuck in at least half the group so that the theater didn't even make any money on us.

There was always a double feature, often a triple feature and sometimes one of those great "dusk-til-dawn" marathons - five monster movies or beach party flicks in a row - enough to test the low threshold of taste of any sixties high schooler.

When The Gemini opened in 1965 it was the largest drive in theater in the world. It was located at the intersection of Central Expressway and Forest. Begun as a twin-screen, a third screen was added later. The complex featured two snack bars, a playground and an outdoor seating area. Other "space age" drive in names soon followed: The Apollo and the Astro.

The Casa View Drive In on Gus Thomasson was opened in 1961. Temporarily shut down in the mid-sixties it re-opened in the summer of 1966 and remained open until the late 70s.

In Person – Frankie Avalon and Deborah Walley were at the Gemini for the premiere of "Beach Blanket Bingo". (They also made an appearance at the Buckner Drive-In that same night.)

Classic Drive-In Features

Movies we watched at local Dallas Drive-Ins of the era

The Notorious Twin East Drive-In

The "notorious" Twin East Drive-in opened on June 24 1955, along side the less-notorious Twin West on Highway 80 (Davis Blvd) in far Oak Cliff (actually in Grand Prairie.) When opened it was the Dallas area's first twin screen drive-in and specialized in standard movie fare. By the early sixties through the end of the decade the East screen began showing risqué flicks that were considered very adult for the time. The West screen began specializing in horror and rock and roll movies.

The fact that the movies could be seen from the highway caused the theater no end of legal trouble and motorists no end of dangerous conditions. It was reported that several cars ran off the road while staring up at the screen and many accidents were attributed to the movies.

As the legal battle raged, a prominent Doctor testified that showing risqué movies along a highway posed a major traffic danger. However, Grand Prairie police testified that the traffic problem was way overstated.

Even though the theater owners promised they would stop showing the naughty pics two weeks later they were running "The Bellboy and The Playgirls". Ultimately, Judge Sarah T. Hughes (who would later administer the oath of office to President Lyndon Johnson) ruled that the movies could continue to be shown. A decade later the films shown at the Lone Star Drive-In made the Twin East's offerings look quaint and innocent by comparison.

The Sports Report – The 60's

Cowboys vs. Texans

Lamar Hunt, son of billionaire Dallas oil tycoon H.L. Hunt was a football fan. He wanted an NFL franchise, but the snooty big league thought that Dallas was beneath them in status and decided to stick with the sophisticated large cities. There were no NFL teams in the sticks of the South and the geniuses of the NFL decided to keep it that way.

So Lamar Hunt went out and founded the AFL – The American Football League (which is now called 'half of the NFL'). He started by creating the hometown team he wanted in the first place. He called them The Dallas Texans.

(Not to be confused with the half-season 1952 NFL team The Texans who became the Baltimore Colts before moving again to Indianapolis. Possibly the low, low turnout for the 1952 team persuaded the NFL that football would never go in Texas. The low turnout could also possibly be blamed on the fact that the 1952 Texans were a really terrible team.)

The first AFL teams created prior to the kickoff in 1960 included a Minneapolis team which was stolen by the NFL in an attempt to cripple the new league prior to the first season. That team became the Minnesota Vikings.

The teams that actually played that very first season in the AFL were the Dallas Texans, The Houston Oilers, The Los Angeles Chargers, The New York Titans, The Boston Patriots, The Denver Broncos, The Buffalo Bills and The Oakland Raiders. All eight teams still exist although the Chargers moved to San Diego, the Texans became the Kansas City Chiefs and the Titans were renamed The Jets.

The AFL teams were considered "a heckuva lot more fun" – at least by the beer-filled guy that sat next to me and my buddy Dave at a Texans game in 1960. It was really true. The AFL, having nothing else really going for it, encouraged its teams to put on a show. Compared to the stodgy "three yards and a cloud of dust" NFL, the new league was a breath of fresh air. To me and all my buddies in the 7th grade, the NFL was the league of old, fat guys and the AFL was the team of today.

Needless to say the NFL really, really hated the new guys. It took a decade and a Joe Namath / Jets victory in an early Super Bowl to bring parity and a merger to the two leagues.

Meanwhile, in a second attempt to foil the new league the stuffy old NFL decided that a team in Dallas was a pretty good idea after all. Hence The Dallas Cowboys. The Cowboys and The Texans shared the Cotton Bowl, with every-other-week games for each team. The Texans literally gave away tickets, and so my friends and I were there for every home game.

The Texans rewarded us with some really fun, run-and-gun football that converted a generation of Dallas baseball fans into pro-football fans overnight. The running of "Little" Abner Haynes electrified us. Fullback Jack Spikes (maybe the greatest name for a running back, ever) and receiver Chris Burford were the other offensive stars on the team. And if you were looking for colorful football names...how about Buffalo Napier, Sherrill Hedrick, Smokey Stover and Cotton Davidson?

<u>Texans trivia</u>: Local musician, banjo king and owner of the The Levee Club in Dallas, Ed Bernet, was on the roster that first year as a receiver. He didn't play much and left after the first season to go into his successful career as a Dallas music superstar.

The first year The Texans had a winning season and finished second in the AFL West. The Cowboys didn't win a single game that first year...who do you think were the local heroes?

In 1962, in the longest championship game in pro-football history, our Dallas Texans beat The Houston Oilers in a double-overtime victory. In the local excitement, the low-scoring, oft-losing, slow-moving Cowboys became the "Dallas Who?" And the NFL started to notice.

Prior to the 1963 season, The Texans snuck off to Kansas City and became The Chiefs. Apparently there was a profit motive, as The Texans had not made any of that in Dallas. It took a couple of years before we all got over our collective pout and began to embrace The Cowboys as our home team. As for me I would trade a full season of The Cowboys to see that one game in 1961 when Abner Haynes dazzled us with five running touchdowns.

Abner Haynes, the first Dallas pro-football superstar.

The AFL Champions in 1962

Cowboys Become the Only Game in Town

When the Texans bolted for KC, we decided to at least give the Cowboys a second glance. After a few years and a few major acquisitions (Don Meredith, Bob Hayes, Don Perkins, et al), The Cowboys became our team (later America's Team) and The Chiefs were just some team from somewhere else. By the late '60s The 'Boys were not only acceptable to us all, they were actually really, really good.

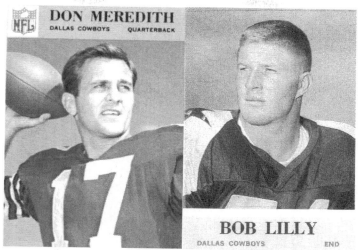

Superstars of the Sixties' Cowboys

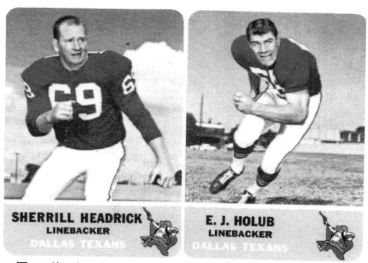

Two linebackers extraordinaire of The Texans.

They Fought Like Cats and Birds

The Fort Worth Cats and The Dallas Eagles rivalry was equal to the SMU / TCU competition for hearts and minds in the area. The two minor-league baseball teams always drew a crowd, in person and on the air, whenever they went head-to-head.

The Eagles had begun back near the turn of the 20th Century and had been know as The Griffins, The Steers, The Giants and The Submarines before settling on The Eagles for the decade of the fifties. The Cats began as the Panthers (a tribute to Fort Worth's nickname of "Panther City") and by the fifties The Eagles / Cats were a firm part of the local sports scene.

Burnett Field in Oak Cliff (named for Eagles owner Dick Burnett) was home field for The Eagles until 1960 when the newly renamed Dallas / Fort Worth Rangers were formed from the Eagles and The Cats' merger.

Eagles Aces: Pitchers Joe Kotrany
and Tommy Bowers.

The Restaurants We Loved

The Classic Argument: El Fenix or El Chico?

El Fenix was the first – founded in 1918 by Mike Martinez, it remained in the family for 90 years. The first El Chico opened on Oak Lawn in 1940, operated by the Cuellar family of Dallas.

The debate was which restaurant had the best Tex-Mex food. That debate still rages in the North Texas area.

Not only did El Fenix have Live Mexican Charros playing every night, but a 65¢ special on Wednesday Nights in the sixties. But then, so did El Chico.

In Casa Linda Plaza the classic El Fenix is still there. (The 65¢ special is not.)

EL FENIX CAFE
OF OAK CLIFF
W-4050 - 120 E. Colorado
DALLAS, TEXAS

MEXICAN FOOD
★ AND
american
TOO!

Thick, juicy steaks
and other
delicious American dishes
at El Chico's famous
popular prices

DELICIOUS BREADED VEAL CUTLET
Tender Cooked with Cream
Gravy, Crisp Fried Potatoes.
Only **$1.10**
★
**BROILED FILET MIGNON
WRAPPED WITH BACON**
Melt in Your Mouth Tenderness! Includes
truly reared green salad with special dress-
ings, and a big potato baked to a turn.
Only **$2.50**
★
FAMOUS EL CHICO ENCHILADA DINNER
Two Big Enchiladas graced with tasty El Chico Chili.
Generous helpings of fried rice and fried beans.
Crisp toasted or plain tortillas.
Only **$1.30**

★ 707 Preston Royal
Village
★ 168 Inwood Village
★ 2931 Abrams Road
★ 110 W. Davis

El Chico
RESTAURANTS

ENJOY EL CHICO MEXICAN FOODS AT HOME, TOO!
Available at your supermarket.

your table
Señor
at
el fenix
Restaurants

FINEST IN
MEXICAN FOOD
STEAKS ● CHICKEN
Since 1918

OAK CLIFF 120 E. COLORADO BLVD.	CASA LINDA 255 CASA LINDA PLAZA
NORTHWEST-HILLCREST NORTHWEST HWY.	LEMMON-INWOOD 5621 LEMMON AVE.
DOWNTOWN 1608 McKINNEY (Between Troubadours Pearl & Akard)	LONGVIEW, TEXAS 1601 U.S. HWY. 259

Hamburger Hangouts

Charco's, The Prince of Hamburgers, The Pig Stand, Krystal, Hardee's, Griff's, Jack In The Box, The Dairy Queen, Goffs, Sivils, The DairyEtte and of course Kips.

The Perfect Restaurant for a Saturday Night After-the-Movie Date was always KIP'S.

At this point in the late fifties when this menu was printed, the combination plate was just 65¢. (A Big Boy, fries and a salad.) That wonderful after-the-date hot fudge sundae – just 35¢. If you'd had a good week baby-sitting or carrying out groceries at Minyard's you might even spring for the full Spencer Steak Dinner – just a buck and a half.

Underwood's Barbecue, Bob White's Barbecue, Fred's Barbecue, DeGeorge's, Red Bryan's, Sonny Bryan's, Lobello's and Joe Moseley's. Dallas was never short for barbecue.

Restaurants We Miss
Bedford's Steak House
Brockles (home of the "special dressing")
Charcos Hamburgers
The China Clipper
The Circle Inn
Dobbs House
Here 'Tis Hamburgers
Jamie's Hamburgers
Joe Moseley's Barbecue
Kip's
La Tunisia
Little Bit o' Sweden
Luby's Cafeteria
Lucas B&B
The Orange Inn
Phil's Delicatessen
The Pig Stands
Poco Taco
Ports o' Call
Sammy's
Shanghai Jimmy's
Topper Restaurants
The Torch
The Town and Country
Wyatt's Cafeteria
Youngblood's Fried Chicken
Zuider Zee

Ports o' Call

Sivil's Drive-In was an Oak Cliff tradition.

Wow…here are some restaurant memories. Third from the bottom on the right – Brockles. How many of you remember Brockles Special Dressing in jars from the grocery store? On a salad, on a cracker or just spooned straight out of the jar. Ymmmm….

Three Dallas classics – Southern Kitchen, The House of Steaks and The Pig Stand.

For most of us of dating age in the 50's and 60's La Tunisia was way out of our price range. But it was sometimes a special occasion out with the family, when Dad was paying.

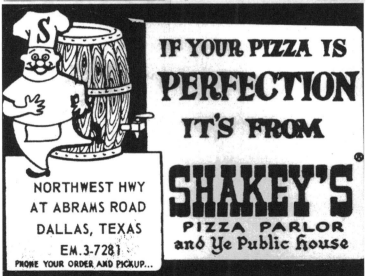
180

The World's Largest Salad Bar Featured At Bedford's Steak House

The entire family enjoys dining out at Bedford's Steak House, Garland Road at Alvin Street. Featuring the world's largest salad bar, Lee Bedford has just opened a new dining room and can accommodate as many as 600 diners. Choose as many salads as you like from over 50 offered while your charcoal steak, ribs or fish is being prepared. Phone 327-2900 for reservations or for party information.

In East Dallas, Bedford's Steak House was one of the finest restaurants of the 50's and 60's. It began as The Casa Linda Lodge, and advertised "The World's Largest Salad Bar."

As kids, one of the fun things at Kips was the free comic book they gave you. (I know it says 10¢ but they were free, honest.) Later as teenagers Kip's became a major after-date gathering spot. (Combination plate: 65¢. Hot Fudge Sundae: 35¢.)

Three Chords and a Cloud of Dust
Dallas Music Scene of the Sixties

The Top Ten Dallas Rock Bands of the Era

The Nightcaps

Beginning in the late fifties, this Dallas white r&b band set the standard for almost every southern garage band to come. The kings of the frat dance, junior high hop, bowling alley blast, and nightclub stage, they released three singles and an impressive album in the late fifties and early sixties. *Wine Wine Wine*, their best known song, was loosely based on the old blues song *Wine Spo Dee O Dee*, and was a big hit in Texas. Every frat and school band had to know it in order to work. It was the pre-Louie Louie essential rock band song of the south. *Twenty Four Hours* (a re-working of the Hank Ballard song *It's Love Baby*) and *Thunderbird* followed, the latter being a raucous celebration of the brand of wine mentioned in the title. You will find covers of these songs by sixties garage bands throughout the world.

A hard-working and much traveled party band, The Nightcaps survived well into the sixties, still playing their brand of frantic frat party music, even when other Texas bands had adopted names like "Oxford Circus" and "The Cicadelics". Members: Billy Joe Shine (vocals), Jack Allday (drums), Mario Daboub (bass), Gene Haufler (guitar) and David Swarz (lead guitar).

Southwest FOB

Starting as a straight up garage band, Theze Few, they morphed into a pseudo-psychedelic style. England Dan (Dan Seals) and John Ford Coley (John Colley) were in this band from Samuel High School.

The Briks

Led by guitarist Richard Borgens and lead singer Cecil Cotton, they recorded *Can You See Me* and *Foolish Baby*.

The Chaparrals

Featuring Jamie Bassett on bass and vocals, The Chaparrals were a hot frat-party attraction and the house band at The Pirates Nook club.

The Chessmen

From Dallas. Featured Jimmie Vaughan (future Fabulous Thunderbirds) and Doyle Bramhall Sr.

The Five Americans

"I See The Light!" was their first big hit. They were the house band at The Pirate's Nook just before The Chaparrals. The Five Americans scored a hug national hit in 1967 with *Western Union*.

Kenny and the Kasuals

From Dallas. Kenny Daniel, David "Bird" Blachley, Lee Lightfoot, Tommy Nichols (replaced by Jerry Smith), Paul Roach. *Nothin' Better To Do*, their first single was written by Daniel and Nichols in ten minutes on the outside steps of The Studio Club. It had the perfect teen attitude about love and romance – "I'll keep loving you only because I have nothing better to do". After a few additional singles and a popular local album entitled "Impact", the band went psychedelic with a mind blower called *Journey To Tyme*. Their "Impact" album has become one of the most highly prized of collectible rock albums, partially because of its incredible rarity and partly because it's filled with garage band standards – cover songs of teen-band hits like *Money* and *Gloria*.

Live at the Studio Club – Kenny and the Kasuals

The Outcasts
Featuring Marc Benno.

Mouse and the Traps
From Dallas. Beg Borrow and Steal, Public Execution and others. Featuring North Texas guitar legend Bugs Henderson and Ronnie "Mouse" Weiss on vocals. Mouse had a Dylanesque voice which became closer to a straight imitation. The Traps also backed up Dallas DJ Jimmy Rabbitt on his recordings and live shows.

The Mystics
From South Oak Cliff High School, their big regional hit was *Didn't We Have a Good Time*.

The Floyd Dakil Four
From Dallas. They recorded *Bad Boy*, *Dance Franny Dance* and others.

Other popular Dallas bands in the mid-sixties included The Cavemen, The Novas, Kit and the Outlaws, The In Crowd, The Warlocks, The Gentlemen, The Five of a Kind, The Demolitions, The Excells, The Jackals and The Marksmen.

The Mystics – from South Oak Cliff High School

For The Record...Big Hits from Big D

Local area rock and roll acts that achieved regional or national hit records in the sixties included:

Bruce Channel. His giant international hit "Hey Baby" (1962) was recorded in Fort Worth

Rick and the Keens out of Fort Worth who had a hit with their re-make of "Peanuts".

The Five Americans – "I See The Light" (1966) and "Western Union" (1967) (below left)

Jon and Robin – "Do It Again" (1967)

Scotty McKay – "Batman" (1966)

Mouse and the Traps – (featuring Bugs Henderson) "Pubic Execution" (1966)

Paul and Paula – "Hey Paula" (1963) recorded in Fort Worth (Shown above right)

Sam The Sham and the Pharaohs – "Wooly Bully" (1965)

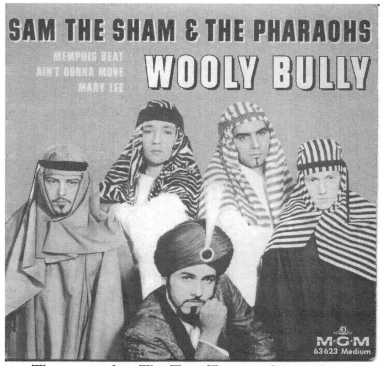

SAM THE SHAM & THE PHARAOHS

MEMPHIS BEAT
AIN'T GONNA MOVE
MARY LEE

WOOLY BULLY

M·G·M
63623 Médium

They started as The Tom Toms and were the house band at the Guthrie Club. By 1965 they were Sam the Sham and the Pharaohs and had the top song of the year.

Teen Clubs, Hangouts and Music Memories

The Studio Club

On Sherry Lane in Preston Center, the Studio Club may not have been Dallas' first Teen Club – certainly not our first regular teen dance spot – but when it opened in 1965, the club immediately became the most popular teen nightclub in town. Located basically in the center of town, it was close enough to everyone from Oak Cliff to Casa Linda.

STUDIO CLUB OF DALLAS

6135 SHERRY LANE IN PRESTON CENTER

THE TEEN NITE CLUB IN DALLAS

The club was much more upscale than your standard roller rink rock hall, it featured the city's top live bands and a strict no-alcohol policy which was ignored by everyone.

The Pit

Located inside of the giant Bronco Bowl facility in Oak Cliff, the Pit was a real night club, with everything but the booze. With a big stage, good acoustics, attractive décor and a quality dance floor, the Pit was rivaled only by the elegant North Dallas Studio Club.

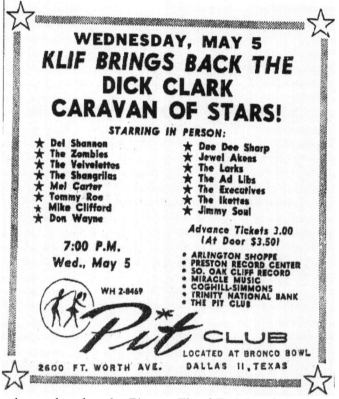

The house band at the Pit was Floyd Dakil and the Pitmen, but other top-level area bands played there as well as national touring shows like the Dick Clark Caravan of Stars seen in the ad above.

Surfers A-Go-Go

In the mid-60's a bowling alley on C.F. Hawn Freeway at Raynelle Avenue became Dallas' newest teen nightclub – Surfer's A-Go-Go. The Cavemen and Johnny Green and the Green Men were regulars and superstars like Chuck Berry were brought in on special occasions to liven up the boxoffice.

The Hullabaloo Teen Scene

GIANT SUMMER OPENING

HULLABALOO™

TEEN SCENE

Young Adults 14-20

Admission Always $1

THURSDAYS BIG OPENING THE **FANTASTIKS**
JUNE 1

FRIDAY THE **BRIKS**
JUNE 2

SATURDAY **KENNY and**
JUNE 3 **the KASUALS**

GIGANTIC SHOW AND DANCE

In 1963 two very different concerts were presented.

Fabian . . . Due in Dallas with the Caravan of Stars for Aug. 5 shows.

Fabian Due For Dallas At The Pit

Fabian will be the headline attraction on the Dick Clark Caravan of Stars which will be presented in two performances at The Pit on Wednesday, Aug. 5.

Performance times at the teen-age night club are 7 p.m. for the public and at 9:30 p.m. for Pit members only. Ticket prices for the public are $3.50, with a cut to $3 for advance sale. Pit members will pay $2.50. A maximum of 1,500 tickets will be sold for each performance, the capacity of the Bronco Bowl, the club headquarters at 2600 Fort Worth Avenue.

In addition to Fabian, other acts will be Gene Pitney, Major Lance, The Crystals, The Coasters, Mike Clifford, Dean & Jean, The Dixie Cups, Brenda Holloway, Brian Hyland, the Kasuals, George McCannon, The Reflections, The Rip Chords, Round Robin, The Shirelles, The Supremes and Donna Loren, the Dr. Pepper Girl.

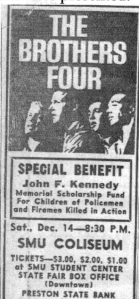

THE BROTHERS FOUR

SPECIAL BENEFIT

John F. Kennedy
Memorial Scholarship Fund
For Children of Policemen
and Firemen Killed in Action

Sat., Dec. 14—8:30 P.M.

SMU COLISEUM

TICKETS—$3.00, $2.00, $1.00
at SMU STUDENT CENTER
STATE FAIR BOX OFFICE
(Downtown)
PRESTON STATE BANK

Fabian, Gene Pitney, The Supremes, Major Lance, Bryan Hyland, The Crystals and others headlined the Dick Clark Caravan of Stars Show at The Pit.

In December folk group The Brothers Four gave a benefit concert in memory of the slain President Kennedy.

Trivia: The Brothers Four big hits included "The Green Leaves of Summer". Bryan Hyland's biggest hit was "Itsy Bitsy Teeny Weeny Yellow Polka Dot Bikini".

LouAnn's

LouAnn's was a club that had been around for a quite a while and made the transition to rock and roll very successfully. Located at the corner of Lovers Lane and Greenville Avenue, it was one of the oldest standing clubs in the city at the time. The club was not run by a person named LouAnn, but by Ann Bovis and her husband Lou (hence "LouAnn's"). LouAnn's was a giant barn of a place with fairly good acoustics and a huge wooden dance floor. It opened on June 8, 1940 and was originally a home to big bands and famous performers. Through the 1940's it was a very popular local dance hall, featuring a wide variety of different acts from crooners and big bands to blues artists and country performers.

By 1960 though, LouAnn's was alternating big band singers with rock and blues bands. Bo Diddley, Chuck Berry and Jimmy Reed were booked regularly into the large venue, while the next attraction might have been Les Elgart and his Orchestra or crooner Mark Dinning. In the mid-sixties the place had become virtually an exclusive venue for local rockers. New Year's Eve 1966 found The Chessmen, The Reasons Why and Theze Few entertaining. In 1967 the club began booking "psychedelic" acts, the first place in Dallas to do so.

Other music clubs in Dallas where the younger crowd went included The Fog, The Phantasmagoria, The Ali Baba, The Losers Club, The Three Thieves and The Pirate's Nook.

Rock and Roller Rinks and Rec Center Rock

All over town roller rinks gave up weekend nights to teenage dance parties. Usually the admission was 25¢ and soft drinks were a dime. Live bands performed from 8PM to Midnight. In Mesquite Broadway Skateland became "Broadway Skateland and Sock Hop A-Go-Go" on weekends. In Pleasant Grove, The Twilight Skating Palace had weekend dances, with local band The Shade playing there most often. The Shamrock Roller rink in nearby Lancaster was another in the long list of rock-and-roller rinks in the area.

Other local rinks included White Rock Skating Rink, Jack and Jills, Dal-Kliff Roller Rink, The Fair Park Skating Rink and Dal-Hi Skating.

The same held true at neighborhood recreation centers. In 1963 – 1964 a regular dance was held at the Harry Stone Rec Center in East Dallas that attracted a thousand kids each night. The dance was called "DreamAires" and the best bands in Dallas played there. All for a 25¢ admission.

And how about the high school gym dances...

Kenny and the Kasuals rock a Dallas high school gym in 1965

Dallas high schools of the 50s and 60s:

Bryan Adams
W.H. Adamson
Crozier Tech
Hillcrest
Thomas Jefferson
Justin F. Kimball
Lincoln
James Madison
North Dallas
L.G. Pinkston
F.D. Roosevelt
W.W. Samuel
H. Grady Spruce
South Oak Cliff
Sunset
Booker T. Washington
W.T. White
Woodrow Wilson

Sump'n Else

Sump'n Else, a live five day-a-week afternoon show on Channel 8 was a local teen dance and music program. Originating in the WFFA remote studio at NorthPark Mall, the show was hosted by Dallas music personality Ron Chapman (shown below).

In addition to the local teenage dancers rockin' out to recorded music, Sump'n Else featured local rock bands, many receiving their first and only TV exposure on the show. Groups like Kenny and the Kasuals, The Briks and The Novas gained local exposure with appearances on Sump'n Else. The show was live and the director would daringly take live shots of the teens outside a large window looking into the studio. This backfired when a student who attended my high school (who I can only remember by the name of "Scar") gave the finger to Dallas on live TV from that spectator window.

DFWs Greatest Hits – More Music Info

From the early days of the recording industry to the present, some very impressive songs have been created and/or recorded in the Dallas - Fort Worth Metroplex. Many of these songs went on to become national and international hits. Some simply reached the attention of local fans and radio stations only. Some of these songs were recorded by Dallas area artists using facilities in other cities, but most were recorded in the DFW Metroplex.

Batman – Scotty McKay (his other local hits included
   Rollin' Dynamite)
Big Blue Diamonds – Gene Summers (his other local hits
   included *Nervous* and *School of Rock and Roll"*)
Blue – LeAnn Rimes (written by Dallas legend Bill Mack)
Chattanooga Choo Choo – Tex Beneke (with Glenn Miller
   Orchestra) Tex was a Fort Worth native who found fame
   as a singer and instrumentalist in the 40s
Cotton Eyed Joe – Adolph Hofner, recorded in Dallas
Cowboys From Hell – Pantera
Crazy Arms – Ray Price
Dance Franny Dance – The Floyd Dakil Combo
Deep Ellum Blues – Blind Lemon Jefferson
Didn't We Have A Good Time – The Mystics
Dis A Itty Bit – Robin Hood Brians (perhaps best known as
   a Dallas area music producer/songwriter)
Disco Lady – Johnnie Taylor
Do It Again (Just a Little Bit Slower) – Jon And Robin and the
In Crowd
Equal Scary People – Sara Hickman
Everybody Clap Your Hands – The Levee Singers (featuring

Ed Bernet, Ronnie Dawson and Smokey Montgomery)

Four on the Floor – The Shutdowns (featuring Scotty McKay and Kirby St. Romaine)

Hey Baby – Bruce Channel (recorded in Fort Worth)

Hey Paula – Paul and Paula (originally known as Jill and Ray)

Hey Suzanne – Bob Haydon

Hide Away – Freddy King

I See The Light – The Five Americans (their big national hit was *Western Union*)

If I Had A Hammer – Trini Lopez (The Dallas native recorded in Los Angeles)

If You Really Want Me To I'll Go – The Rondels (Delbert McClinton was the lead singer of this Fort Worth band)

If You've Got The Money Honey – Lefty Frizzell (written and recorded at Beck's Studio in Dallas)

Impact – Kenny and the Kasuals (this mid-sixties album of cover songs was once listed in Rolling Stone magazine as one of the ten most collectible U.S. albums of all time)

Journey To Tyme – Kenny and the Kasuals

Kiss An Angel Good Morning – Charley Pride

Legs – ZZ Top (two thirds of this "little ol' band from Texas" are Dallasites)

Let Them Talk – Bobby Patterson

Lido Shuffle – Boz Scaggs (attended high school at St. Marks in Dallas)

Linda Lu – Ray Sharpe

Lookin' Out The Window – Written by Doyle Bramhall, recorded by Stevie Ray Vaughan both of Dallas.

My Blue Heaven – Gene Austin (the Dallas-area native) introduced this classic back in the twenties)

On and On – Erykah Badu

Psychotic Reaction – Positively 13 O'Clock

A Public Execution – Mouse and the Traps
They May Not Be My Toes – Whistlin' Alex Moore
Tightrope – Stevie Ray Vaughan and Double Trouble
Rockin' Bones – Ronnie Dawson
Smell of Incense – Southwest FOB
Somethin' I Said – Lew Williams (who also
    wrote and recorded *Cat Talk*).
Soul Serenade – King Curtis
Stay – Lisa Loeb
Stoned – The Old 97s
Stormy Monday Blues – T-Bone Walker
Summer's Coming – Kirby St. Romaine
Tchaikovsky's Piano Concerto Number 1 – Van Cliburn
Ten Long Fingers – "Groovey" Joe Poovey
Theme From Elvira Madigan – Don "Jake" Jacoby
There's Your Trouble – Dixie Chicks
Tuff Enuff – The Fabulous Thunderbirds.
    (Lead guitarist Jimmie Vaughan is from Dallas.)
Walkin' With Frankie – Frankie Lee Sims
Welcome to Hollywood – Mark Benno (with Leon Russell)
What I Am – Edie Brickell and New Bohemians
Wine Wine Wine – The Nightcaps (the single and the album
    of the same name)
Wooly Bully – Sam the Sham and the Pharaohs

**Recorded songs about Dallas from the 1920s
through 2000 include:**

Big D – From the soundtrack of *The Most Happy Fella*
  (by Frank Loesser)
Big D Blues – Hot Lips Page
Bid D Boogie Woogie – Reverend Horton Heat
Big D Shuffle – Bugs Henderson
Big D Woman – Mac Curtis
Dallas – Joe Ely, Butch Hancock, The Flatlanders and
  others (written by Jimmie Dale Gilmore)
Dallas – Other songs named *Dallas* have also been recorded
  by Willie Nelson, Johnny Winter, Floyd Cramer, Steely
  Dan, Jimmy Buffet, Billie Jo Spears, Poco, Alan Jackson,
  David Byrne and others
Dallas Alice – Sir Douglas Quintet
Dallas Blues – Floyd Dixon, Louis Armstrong, Link Wray,
  Woody Herman, Fats Waller and others
Dallas County Blues – Gene Autry
A Dallas Cowboy and a New Orleans Saint – The Kendalls
Dallas Cowboys – Charlie Pride
Dallas Darlin' – Tom Jones
Dallas Darling – Tex Ritter
Dallas Days and Fort Worth Nights – Chris LeDoux
Dallas Doings – Duke Ellington
Dallas (For You My Love) – Ray Sharpe
Dallas Man – Georgia White
The Dallas Morning News – Red Steagall
Dallas Rag – The Dallas String Band
Dance Franny Dance – Floyd Dakil Combo
A Date In Dallas – Del Reeves
Deep Ellum Blues – Blind Lemon Jefferson
Deep Ellum Boogie – Willie Willis
The Devil Lives in Dallas – Rusty Weir

Don't Go To Dallas – Joe Tex
Down Dallas Alley – Buckwheat Zydeco
Elm Street Blues – Texas Bill Day
Fort Worth and Dallas Blues – Huddie "Leadbelly" Ledbetter
Full Moon Over Dallas – Mike Morgan and The Crawl
Goin' To Dallas – Lightnin' Hopkins
Goin' Up To Dallas – Leon's Lone Star Cowboys
The Good Old Dallas Cowboys – Waylon Jennings
Goodnight Dallas – Carlene Carter
Here I Am In Dallas – Faron Young
He's In Dallas – Reba McEntire
Houston, Dallas and San Antone – David Allen Coe
I Ain't Leavin' Dallas – Dave and Sugar
I Always Die In Dallas – Will Barnes
If You're Ever Down In Dallas – Lee Ann Womack
I Had A Ball In Big D – Artist unknown
I Lost Her To A Dallas Cowboy – Moe Bandy
I'm In Love and He's In Dallas – Tanya Tucker
Interurban Blues – Billiken Johnson
I Walked From Dallas – Howlin' Wolf
McKinney Street Stomp – Joe Pullum
That Dallas Man – Mae West, Benny Goodman, and others
This Ain't Dallas – Hank Williams Jr.
Trinity River Blues – T-Bone Walker
West Dallas Drag – Joe Pullum
West Dallas Woman – Joe Pullum
What's The Matter With Deep Elm? – Moon Mullican
Who Do I Know In Dallas? – Willie Nelson
Who Stole The Marker From The Grave of Bonnie Parker? –
    Gene Summers

KBOX *presented Sonny and Cher. KLIF presented*
The Beach Boys. The two stations not only battled for
ratings and listeners they also fought to see
which station could land the best concerts.

Meanwhile local bands like Kit and The Outlaws
above, not only opened for Sonny and Cher, but filled
gyms, roller rinks and teen clubs all over town.

203

When The Beatles Came To Town

The Beatles have a Sept. 18 date looming at Dallas Memorial Auditorium. The famed rock 'n' rollers will strip off here as a part of a 23-city tour and 55,000 fans are expected to pack the arena for the appearance.

I bought two tickets. I think they cost $2 each. Somebody at school the week before the concert offered me $5 for each ticket — a clear profit of six bucks. I sold the tickets. I am an idiot.

But, a resourceful idiot. My friend Bobby had a connection with the concession stand people at Memorial Auditorium and had gotten on as a popcorn seller for the event. His job was to walk up and down the aisles, before and during the concert selling the stuff. Of course he had no intention of selling anything at least while The Beatles themselves were performing. Oh, he might sell a few before the concert and he might even act like he was in business during the opening acts (The Bill Black Combo, The Exciters, Clarence 'Frogman' Henry, and Jackie DeShannon), but popcorn was just a dodge to get in the building.

Bobby told me to wait outside a certain door at a certain time and he would let me in. It was perfect! I would see The Beatles and still make a six buck profit!

So on September 18, 1964, there I was standing at the side-back concessionaire door of Memorial Auditorium, right on time, actually about fifteen minutes early. Fifteen minutes came and went and took another fifteen minutes with them.

204

The Beatles' press conference in Dallas, where they were asked the same stupid questions they were asked in every city they visited.

No Bobby. I waited for another thirty minutes. Still no Bobby.

I went around to the front. Crowds were starting to swell. Guys were walking around selling "I Love Paul" pennants (and of course pennants for each of the other Beatles too, but it seemed like he was only moving the Paul ones). Others were selling buttons, shirts, bumper stickers and so on. Someone had bought and dropped a "Beatles Forever" bumper sticker and it had a big footprint in the middle where someone had stepped on it before the owner could retrieve it. It was a light green with big black letters.

Wait a minute! It was *light green*, the same color as the tickets I had bought and stupidly sold. In no time I had grabbed the pennant, carefully torn off a rectangle roughly the size of the tickets, and scratched a bunch of hieroglyphics on it with a nail and some tar off the sidewalk. I looked at my masterpiece. It was the worst forged ticket in the history of forgery.

That didn't matter. My plan was to hand the ticket to the guy and before he could react sprint past him and into the Auditorium where I would hide until the concert started.

I was standing around with a group of kids who were all by one set of doors, which – even though there was no ticket taker inside – we had been assured was one of the entrances. All of a sudden the other group at the main entrance started going in. Our group, all of whom but me had actual tickets, had been duped and we were not at the right door.

Our little crowd began to surge. We pushed against the locked doors which suddenly sprung open to the inside. We were in! While most of the kids looked around to see who to give their tickets to, I hot-footed it to the balcony where I kept changing seats every time the real owner showed up.

Then, the lights went down and The Bill Black Combo was on stage rockin'. I had done it. I saw The Beatles in their only Dallas performance and I made six bucks on the deal.

Later I found out that my friend Bobby had decided to chuck the popcorn ruse altogether, forget about me at the back door and go with a much better plan. He crawled under the makeshift stage, way to the back and hunkered down. The plan was that when The Beatles came on he would somehow work his way to the surface and end up on stage with the lads themselves.

Except that the cops looked under the stage, found Bobby, turned him in to the concession people who confiscated his popcorn, tray and little paper hat and unceremoniously tossed him out. He never saw The Beatles.

And so, after all these decades, all I have to say to my friend Bobby is "Nyah, nyah, nyah, nyah, nyah! I saw The Beatles!"

NORMALCY RETURNS

Dallas Survives Beatles

Dallas has survived the Beatles.

Memorial Auditorium was still standing Saturday morning. No teen-agers were reported missing. No Beatle-working policemen resigned from the force. And the only ones taking a dip in the Cabana Motor Hotel fountain were a couple of sparrows.

Dallas Police Chief Jesse Curry, who attended Friday night's performance both as a parent and as a working officer, complimented the more than 10,000 fans that crowded into the auditorium.

"I'm real proud of our young people," he said. "There was no flagrant misbehavior and they showed that they could enjoy the Beatles without tearing down the place."

"I rather liked them," Curry confessed; "They impressed me as a bunch of fine boys."

Curry talked to them in their dressing rooms after Friday night's show and admitted to a little toe-tapping during their 30-minute performance.

The only place in Dallas still feeling tremors from their visit was the Cabana, where the four Britons stayed.

Cabana executive director Michael Rosenstein said the hotel had been receiving an average of 60 telephone calls an hour from youngsters wanting anything the Beatles touched, walked on or slept in.

"We're not selling anything," Rosenstein said, however. "Everything is back to normal."

Among the gifts presented to the Beatles during their brief stay were 10-gallon hats given them upon their arrival at Love Field by Kathleen Lingo in behalf of the Dallas Civic Opera Association.

"It was mostly for a lark," said Kathleen, a 21-year-old senior at Sarah Lawrence College.

But of the thousands of fans surrounding the famed quartet,

Yolanda Hernandez, president of the Beatle fan club, and her friends claim the most information about them.

"They just love our Texas accents. George can imitate it best.

"Ringo is like a chipmunk and never sits still. And he even likes 'long-hair' music.

"Paul sleeps in red silk pajamas.

"And to comb their hair, they just stand straight and shake like mad and it falls into place.

"They act and look normal just like everyone else."

And maybe Dallas can now return to normal, too.

PC Cobb Stadium, home of high school track meets.
Inside the Love Field Terminal.

Don Meredith of the Dallas Cowboys. The Turnpike. At The Fair: The Hammer

Near the end of 1964, The State Fair Coliseum hosted the All Star Rodeo. I was never quite sure what the term "rip-snortin'" meant, but if I had attended this event I guess I would have found out.

101 Boomer Things To Know About Dallas (and a couple about Fort Worth)

The number one rated radio station for the decade was KLIF 1190.

The first automatic traffic light in America was installed in Dallas.

The first convenience store in the world was in Oak Cliff. The first inconvenience store was in Pleasant Grove. (No, not really.)

The first recordings by The Dixie Chicks, Roy Orbison, The Fabulous Thunderbirds and Vanilla Ice were recorded in Dallas.

The first radio station in Texas was WRR.

The first TV station in Texas was WBAP (OK, we admit it's in Fort Worth, but hey, it comes in nice and clear in Dallas, too.)

The first planned shopping center in America – Highland Park Village.

Liquid Paper was invented in Dallas in 1956 by Bette Nesmith Graham, who is also the mother of Michael Nesmith of The Monkees. She made the first batch in her Dallas kitchen and originally called it "Mistake-Out".

The first of the spectacular "His & Her" gifts offered in the Neiman-Marcus Christmas book appeared in 1960.

When the land for the future NorthPark Mall was acquired, the neighborhood (and former city) known as "Little Egypt" was demolished and the primarily African-American residents were relocated to other homes.

The original Lion's Club was in Dallas.

In 1952 a Dallas woman was sentenced to 13 months for biting two cops.

During 1965 and 1966 KLIF's Jimmy Rabbitt broadcast from a little building on top of the snack bar of the Gemini. They called him "Jimmy at the Gemini".

Lookin' for Tex-Mex cuisine? El Fenix, Chili's, On The Border and El Chico restaurants all began in Dallas. The fajita and the frozen margarita originated in Dallas too.

The first Dave and Buster's and Steak and Ale restaurants were in Dallas.

The world-famous opera stars Joan Sutherland and Placido Domingo each made their first American appearance in Dallas.

The Dallas Civic Opera debuted in 1957. Among the first artists to perform was the internationally famed Maria Callas.

Van Cliburn won the prestigious Tchaikovsky Piano Competition in Moscow in 1958.

The first "Pepsi Challenge" occurred in Dallas (and I was there!)

The transistor radio was invented in Dallas.

And let's not forget the integrated circuit, without which there would be no personal computers, internet, moon landings and a thousand other things that shape our lives.

Dallas legend Blind Lemon Jefferson was the best selling blues recording artist in the country during his era. He passed away in 1929.

On January 2, 1950, the newest member of the Margo Jones Theater joined the troupe. His name was Larry Hagman, and 28 years later he returned to the city to star as "J.R." in the TV series "Dallas".

In their first three games of 1926 The SMU Mustangs football team outscored their opponents by a combined score of 127-0.

Bonnie Parker is buried in Crown Hill Cemetery in Dallas.

Clyde Barrow is buried in Dallas' Western Heights Cemetery. His brother Buck is also buried there.

In 1935 the SMU Mustangs football team was ranked number one in the country and TCU was ranked second.

The reason Dallas calls Pegasus "the flying red horse" is because that's the phrase that was used in The Magnolia Oil Company (and later The Mobil Oil Company) advertising: "Look for the sign of the flying red horse".

Clyde Barrow's middle name was "Chesnut". Bonnie Parker was only 4 foot 10 inches tall.

Growing up together in Fort Worth, future golf champs Byron Nelson and Ben Hogan were caddies at the same golf course.

The Dallas sheriff for much of the 1930s and 1940s was named Smoot Schmid.

The State Fair of Texas actually designated a day in 1923 as Ku Klux Klan Day.

The Dallas Theater Center opened in December of 1959. The building is the only theater ever designed by Frank Lloyd Wright.

In 1929 Bonnie Parker worked as a waitress at Marco's Café in downtown Dallas. At the same time, Clyde Barrow's parents ran a small store on Commerce Street.

The site of the Texas School Book Depository at 411 Elm Street was once owned by Dallas founder John Neely Bryan.

The Cowboys did not win a single regular season game in their first season.

The Slurpee frozen beverage was invented in Dallas and introduced at 7-Eleven Stores in 1966. 150 million were sold in the first year.

How 7-Eleven stores looked in the 50s and 60s.

Six Flags Over Texas is bigger than Disneyland. The "six flags" in the park's name refer to the six countries of which Texas was once a part: Spain, France, Mexico, The Republic of Texas, The Confederacy and The United States.

One of the most prolific of Dallas movie directors was Spencer Williams who later played Andy in the TV series *Amos and Andy*. Two of his many movies made in Dallas were *Blood of Jesus* and *Dirty Gertie of Harlem USA*.

Lucky 13. When the National Football League awarded Dallas a franchise for The Cowboys in 1960, the team became the league's thirteenth team. The franchise cost the Clint Murchison investment group a whopping $600,000. The team is currently valued at over $650,000,000!

WRR in Dallas was the first city-owned radio station in the U.S. to feature entertainment programs.

In 1943-44 White Rock Lake near Winfrey Point was the site of a German Prisoner of War Camp housing captured prisoners from Rommel's Afrika Corps. The camp was located on the site of a former temporary US Army Boot Camp.

The corny dog was invented in Dallas by Neil Fletcher and introduced in 1942 at the Fair Park Midway.

Candy Barr, the famous dancer from the Theater Lounge in downtown, was busted for pot in Dallas way back in 1957.

"The Frito Pie", which originated in Dallas probably in the forties, was not a pie at all. It was a bowl full of chili, Fritos Corn Chips and other stuff fixed like a thick stew.

Preston Road was originally a major part of a primary southwestern Indian trail which ran from south Texas to the present site of St. Louis, Missouri.

In 1954 the entire town of Bisbee, Texas visited the WBAP-TV studios to watch *The Bobby Peters Show*. It is the only recorded time in history when an entire town was in the studio audience of a local TV show.

Prior to his basketball career Dennis Rodman once worked as a janitor at the DFW International Airport.

While passing through Dallas in May of 1958 Buddy Holly and the Crickets stopped at a motorcycle shop in Oak Cliff. They each purchased a motorcycle, which they rode home to Lubbock. (See photo just below)

The Dallas areas of Oak Cliff, East Dallas, Pleasant Grove and Cedar Springs – each was once an independent city. Beginning before the turn of the century with the annexation of East Dallas, by the middle of the 20th Century all of the cities were a part of Dallas.

On September 3, 1955, if you had only known, you could have seen Elvis Presley perform live at a Dallas nightclub called The Round Up. The cover charge was one buck.

In 1958 researchers at Texas Instruments in Dallas invented the integrated circuit. This allowed for the growth of the electronics industry and the introduction of the personal computer.

Perhaps the most notorious of any Dallas nightclub was The Carousel Club, which gained notoriety after its operator, Jack Ruby gunned down Lee Harvey Oswald.

In addition to the Carousel Club, during the decade prior to Kennedy assassination. Jack Ruby also operated a successful Dallas dance club known as "The Silver Spur". It was located on Ervay Street.

Texas war hero and actor Audie Murphy was in town in January of 1952 for the premiere of his latest movie "The Cimarron Kid".

Often described as the first fully enclosed and covered shopping mall in America, Big Town opened in Mesquite just east of Dallas, in 1959.

According to reformer J.T. Upchurch in 1912, the noted and respected Dallas doctor and civic leader W.W. Samuel (for whom the high school was named) owned a certain property near downtown which was being operated as "an immoral resort". There was no claim that Samuel was aware of the use of the rental property.

The Republic Bank Building opened in 1954, becoming the tallest building in the city at the time. The revolving light at the top of the tower could be seen all over Dallas.

During 1949 an average of five new businesses opened each day in Dallas.

In 1956 the annual State Fair of Texas featured two important events: a live performance by Elvis Presley and the opening of the Monorail ride. The Monorail continued in service until the mid-sixties. Elvis was just a one-day deal at the Fair.

The Monorail debuted at the Fair in 1956

Here's an interesting fact – there aren't actually 101 facts in this listing. At least I don't think there are. I'm not going to count them…are you?

The Cotton Bowl became known as "The House That Doak Built" after the popularity of the SMU star caused the facility to be expanded.

In 1957 Trammell Crow and John Stemmons, opened the Home Furnishings Mart. Eventually the center becomes The Dallas Market Center, the largest wholesale sales and merchandise facility in the world.

During World War I, Love Field was used as a U.S. aviation training facility. At the same time, Fair Park became the site of Camp Dick, an army training camp.

High tech aircraft stands ready at Love Field to repulse an attack by enemy Zeppelins. If it wasn't for these brave aviators, Bachman Lake could have been overrun by the Huns.

Big Tex actually began life as a huge statue of Santa. In 1952 the 52-Foot tall Texas cowboy, made his debut as the "official greeter" of the State Fair. He had a very weird, creepy look in his eyes then,  even more inappropriate for Santa, but still too strange for a cowboy. Soon after, his entire head was redone. Below we see them either beheading him or heading him. Not sure which. But check out those creepy eyes!

Disclaimer, Sincere Apology and Denial

Every word in this document is true, except for the stuff I made up, which is a fairly hefty portion, I'll admit. But some of the rest is factual, or at least based on solid rumors and/or possible hearsay. Some of the remainder of the information is pure b.s. In fact a bunch of it is. Actually I think everything in the book is true. But what do I know?

Ten bucks says you haven't read this far in the document. If you actually read this, let me know and I'll be shocked. But I won't actually give you the ten bucks.

Also I didn't actually count the "101 Boomer Things To Know". If you did, consider getting a life.

If anyone is upset by anything at all in this book, then I hereby deny that I had anything to do with it and in fact will swear that I didn't even live here then. I will without hesitation deny all knowledge of everything that ever existed, and in a court of law will swear that you are actually responsible for whatever it is you're upset about, not me.

In other words, if you don't like it, you are cordially invited to bite me.

If, on the other hand, you are enchanted by this humble volume of memories then thank you so very much and may you always have blue skies and green lights.

Recommended Reading

Information for this book came from decades of reading and researching publications such as The Dallas Morning News, The Dallas Times Herald, Broadcasting Magazine, Boxoffice Magazine, Billboard Magazine, D Magazine, Goldmine Magazine, The Dallas Observer and many other publications. Many of the stories and recollections in the book came from the memory of the author and his friends.

Although material in this book did not necessarily come from any of the following books, here is a list of 'Recommended Reading' for a good background on Dallas pop culture history.

STOMP AND SHOUT, The All-Too-Real Story of Kenny and the Kasuals and the Garage Band Revolution of the 60s. By Richard Parker and Kenny Daniel. Oomph Media LLC, 2011.

The Unauthorized History of Dallas. By Rose-Mary Rumbley Eakin Press, 1991.

The Book of Dallas. By Evelyn Oppenheimer and Bill Porterfield (Editors)

The Great State Fair of Texas – An Illustrated History. By Nancy Wiley. Taylor Publishing.

Dallas Then and Now (Then & Now) by Ken Fitzgerald

Historic Photos of Dallas by Michael V. Hazel